Barbec

The Cookbook Library

Flame Tree has been creating **family-friendly**, **classic** and **beginner recipes** for our best-selling cookbooks for over ten years now. Our mission is to offer you a wide range of **expert-tested** dishes, while providing **straightforward** step-by-step photos and clear images of the final dish so that you can match it to your own results. Further information is available at **FlameTreeRecipes.com**

Publisher's Note: Raw or semi-cooked eggs should not be consumed by babies, toddlers, pregnant or breast-feeding women, the elderly or those suffering from a recurring illness.

Publisher & Creative Director: Nick Wells
Senior Project Editor: Catherine Taylor
Art Director: Mike Spender
Digital Design & Production: Chris Herbert

Special thanks to Gina Steer for her continued help and contributions, and to Steven Morris and Sally Davis.

This is a **FLAME TREE** Book

FLAME TREE PUBLISHING
Crabtree Hall, Crabtree Lane
Fulham, London SW6 6TY
United Kingdom
www.flametreepublishing.com

Flame Tree is part of The Foundry Creative Media Company Limited

First published 2009

11 13 12
5 7 9 10 8 6 4

ISBN: 978-1-84786-549-6

Printed in China

Barbecue

Quick and Easy, Proven Recipes

**FLAME TREE
PUBLISHING**

Contents

Vegetables **112**

Side Dishes & Salads **132**

Contents

Summer Desserts 222

Summer Drinks 246

Barbecues

An Introduction

Barbecuing is the perfect way to entertain both family and friends. However, sometimes even the most confident person can be put off – who wants to cook in front of an audience and get it wrong? As a result, many barbecues sit on a patio or terrace neglected and forlorn, hardly used except for the occasional sausage. Well read on – this book will change all that. Read this introduction first so you are completely familiar with the basics of barbecuing and have a few trial runs before embarking on a full-scale party.

Choosing Your Barbecue

Before buying, consider which barbecue is right for you. First consider the size – how many will you be cooking for? And how often will you use it? It's not worth spending masses if you are only going to use it occasionally. Where will you use it and store it? Which type of fuel do you favour? And of course, what will you cook? All these points must be considered.

Types of Barbecue

There are six main types of barbecues in varying sizes and prices, all with their pros and cons.

CHARCOAL BARBECUE The traditional choice, there are many charcoal (or wood burning) barbecues to choose from, ranging in price and sophistication. The very simplest consists of a tray on legs with an adjustable grill rack. They can be free-standing or simply placed on a sturdy surface such as a specially built wide wall. The fuel is placed in the tray and lit at least 20–30 minutes before using, or longer. This allows the smoke to disperse and the coals to become hot. The food is placed on the grill rack for cooking.

For more sophisticated barbecues, look for adjustable air vents which help to control the flow of air and thus the temperature. Or check out barbecues which boast a rotisserie and hood, making them ideal for indirect grilling, cooking whole chickens or larger fish.

KETTLE BARBECUES Also free-standing, the domed lid makes kettle barbecues ideal for both grilling and roasting and perfect for cooking whole fish – much in the same way as an oven. Two methods of heating are available, either charcoal or gas-fuelled.

BUILT-IN BARBECUES These barbecues are normally permanent fixtures and are often placed in the garden where there is plenty of room for seating. A chimney can be used to take the smoke away from the immediate area.

GAS BARBECUES

Fuelled normally by bottled butane and propane gas, these consist of a trolley with a thermometer located inside the hood and the gas bottle stored in the cupboard underneath. The grill rack is inset into the trolley with work areas on at least one side but often on both. Often a small burner is on one of the sides for the preparation of sauces. Stir-fries can be cooked on this.

The heat is measured in BTU (British Thermal Units). Look for two elements rather than one as two give a more even distribution of heat; these are made either from stainless steel or iron (remember that iron tends to rust), while lava rock or ceramic stones help prevent the gas jets from becoming blocked with meat juices or fat. The temperature is very easy to control but do ensure that the knobs are sturdy.

ELECTRIC BARBECUES These operate in a very similar manner to the oven in your kitchen. They are the easiest to use and control due to their thermostatic controls, which almost guarantee perfect results every time.

DISPOSABLE BARBECUES These can only be used once and are normally quite small. They consist of a lightweight foil tray filled with charcoal (treated for easy ignition). Check whether you are allowed to use them in your chosen area, as many picnic areas forbid their use. Take care in their disposal.

Types of Fuel

WOOD Hard wood, rather than soft, is best for burning on the barbecue. The smell and taste of foods cooked in wood smoke is wonderful – look for wood that gives off a particular perfume when burning, such as pine. Hickory wood is popular for its flavour. Wood is not that easy to light but burns quickly, so the barbecue quickly becomes cold unless the cooking process is interrupted with more wood being added. Time must be taken for the heat to return.

LUMPWOOD CHARCOAL This is made from wood that has been fired in a kiln. It is extremely easy to light. As it has already reached the charcoal stage there is less waiting than with hard wood. Look for larger pieces rather than the small.

BRIQUETTES These are crushed charcoal, with starch added as a binder, and are an excellent heat source. The best are made from crushed coconut shells as they hold the heat for longer. Some may be 'self lighting' – so-called because paraffin or petroleum has usually been added to aid ignition.

Barbecue Tools

Once you have selected which barbecue is for you, it is time to consider the tools you will require.

TONGS A sturdy pair of tongs is essential – look for ones that have heat-resistant handles and grippers that will not damage the cooked foods. A second pair is good for turning the coals over or helping with the food.

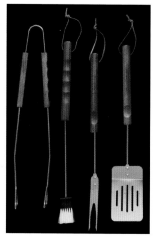

LONG-HANDLED FORK

A long-handled fork is ideal for turning steaks, chops, sausages and all firmer foods. It is also good for checking if the food is cooked.

LONG-HANDLED FISH SLICE

As the name suggests, this is perfect for turning whole fish over. Two is even better.

HINGED BASKETS These are perfect for cooking whole fish, both large and small.

SKEWERS/KEBAB STICKS The long-handled metal skewers are good for firm foods. If using wooden skewers, it is essential that the sticks are soaked in cold water for at least 30 minutes to prevent them from catching alight. It is also a good idea to wrap the handling area in a double piece of kitchen foil so that they can be picked up easily.

GRIDDLES/HOT PLATES/BARBECUE TRAYS You can cook food on these over the barbecue in the same way as you might use a frying pan or griddle on the hob – super for foods that are too fragile to be placed directly on the grill rack.

WIRE BRUSH An essential tool for cleaning the grill rack.

HEAVY-DUTY OVEN GLOVES It is a good idea to wear these to protect your hands from the heat. Separate gloves (as opposed to a linked pair) give greater flexibility when handling a very hot grill rack and tools.

Hints & Tips for Perfect Barbecues

- Before buying, decide what type of barbecue you want, which fuel you prefer and where it is going to be located.
- Make sure that the barbecue is in a stable position, that the smoke will not be swirling around the food or guests, that the area is well lit for visibility and that you have a fire extinguisher or bucket of water nearby, just in case.
- Do not use flammable liquids to ignite the barbecue. If necessary, use 'self lighting' briquettes.
- Flavours can be introduced by using pre-flavoured coals or sprinkling herbs or spices on top of the coals.
- Normally charcoal needs 20–30 minutes' preheating time.
- Wood is perhaps the hardest to regulate and is the most unreliable. The wood needs to burn down until a white or grey ash forms on the coals before using. It can also be sprinkled with flavours. Light about 1 hour before cooking.
- Gas and electric barbecues are easy to regulate and normally do not need to be preheated.
- Never use the barbecue with bare feet and wear an apron to prevent burns to the body.
- Be aware when children and pets are around a hot barbecue and never leave a lit or hot one unattended.
- Clean the barbecue thoroughly once cool and before using again.

Preparation

A little preparing before starting to cook will make life easier, ensure that the barbecue is a success and everyone including the 'chef' has fun.

- Choose meat that does not need long slow cooking – use steaks, ribs or chops.
- To help tenderize and impart more flavour, marinate for at least 30 minutes before cooking. As well as a 'wet' marinade, try a 'rub', which consists of a dry mix usually made from a mixture of spice or dried herbs. Rub this into the food's surface and leave for 30 minutes before cooking. Marinades are also good for whole fish as well as fillets, kebabs, poultry, fruits and vegetables such as peppers, aubergines and courgettes. When ready to cook, remove the marinated food and allow any excess marinade to drip back into the dish rather than on the hot coals. If liked, brush the food lightly with extra marinade during cooking.
- Ensure that poultry and pork are thoroughly cooked. Remember that boneless cuts are quicker to cook than, say, drumsticks.
- Never leave raw foods, especially meats, poultry or salads, in direct sunlight or a warm place for longer than a few minutes. Keep covered in a cool place until ready to serve.
- Use separate utensils, especially pastry brushes, knives and boards, for raw and cooked foods in order to avoid cross contamination.
- Prepare as much as possible ahead of time. This will speed up the cooking once you are ready to start cooking.
- If food is cooking too quickly move it away from the centre, towards the edge of the grill.
- The best way of checking the heat of the charcoal is with the hand. Place your hand above the heat – the longer you can keep it there the cooler the barbecue: 2 seconds = hot, 3–4 seconds = medium hot and 5–6 seconds = low heat.

Note: in the recipes in this book, 'prepare the barbecue' means 'prepare and light the barbecue' – it will depend on which fuel you are using as to how long before cooking you will need to do this. If a recipe asks you to 'prepare a covered' barbecue, this means a kettle barbecue or some sort of barbecue with a hood, to enable you to trap the rising heat and use the barbecue more like an oven. If you do not have a barbecue with a hood, you may be able to cook food in a similar way in foil parcels.

So you have the 'barbie' and the tools; you have the recipes and you know what to do. Happy barbecuing!

Butters, Coatings & Marinades

Dry Coatings

Dry mixtures of breadcrumbs, herbs and spices add flavour and texture to barbecued food. They can also protect the food from the harsh heat of the grill, resulting in a more subtle, grilled flavour. A simple coating of breadcrumbs can keep food moist inside while creating a crisp and crunchy outside. Food coated in a blend of fresh herbs and spices can be left to marinate before cooking. Dry coatings best suit thinner portions that cook quickly so the coatings don't burn. Partially cook longer-cooking foods before coating and grilling them. Try these three different mixtures:

For 2 Fish Fillets
grated rind of 1 lemon or 1 lime
2 tbsp freshly chopped coriander
1 tbsp chopped chervil
sea salt and freshly ground black pepper to taste

For 4 Chicken Breast Fillets
3 tbsp fresh white breadcrumbs
1 small red chilli pepper, seeds removed
    and chopped
2 tbsp chopped basil leaves
grated rind of 1 lime
1 clove garlic, finely chopped
sea salt and freshly ground black pepper to taste

For 450 g/1 lb Beef, Lamb or Pork
1 tsp Chinese five-spice powder
1 tsp sea salt
1 tsp freshly ground black pepper
2 tbsp freshly chopped coriander leaves
1 small red chilli pepper,
    seeded and chopped

Follow these steps when using any dry coating mixture:

1. Brush the food with oil and coat in the prepared mixture.

2. Cook on a preheated oiled barbecue, griddle or grill.

Flavoured Butters

A slice of flavoured butter melting on a hot-from-the-grill piece of fish, chicken, meat or vegetable is a quick and tasty additional seasoning. They can be made up to 3–4 days ahead of time or frozen for up to 2 months. Flavoured butters are rolled into logs, then sliced, scooped or piped onto cooked foods. They are also a delicious spread for warm grilled bread. Follow the steps at the bottom of the page for any of these flavoured butter options.

For 450 g/1 lb Fish or Seafood

OPTION 1
125 g/4 oz softened butter
grated rind and juice of
 1 lime

OPTION 2
125 g/4 oz softened butter
2 tbsp freshly chopped
 coriander
1 tbsp chopped chervil
1 clove garlic, chopped
juice of 1 lemon

For 450 g/1 lb Beef, Lamb or Pork

OPTION 1
125 g/4 oz softened butter
2 tsp chopped rosemary
1 small red chilli pepper,
 seeded and finely chopped
freshly ground black pepper

OPTION 2
125 g/4 oz softened butter
2 cloves garlic, chopped
2 spring onions, finely chopped
freshly ground black pepper

For 450 g/1 lb Chicken

OPTION 1
125 g/4 oz softened butter
2 canned anchovy fillets,
 drained and mashed
juice of 1 lemon
freshly ground black pepper

OPTION 2
125 g/4 oz softened butter
2 cloves garlic, finely
 chopped
1 small green chilli pepper,
 seeded and finely chopped
grated rind and juice of 1 lime

1. Beat the butter until soft, with a spoon or mixer.

2. Add the flavourings and mix well.

3. Spoon onto a piece of clingfilm and shape into a log.

4. Remove the clingfilm and slice into rounds to serve.

Marinades

One of the easiest ways to add flavour and succulence to food before barbecuing is to marinate. Foods can be marinated for a few minutes or up to several hours, and even overnight. The longer the marinating time, the stronger the flavour will be, so don't marinate delicately flavoured foods like fish for too long – 30 minutes is usually sufficient. At least 3 hours is recommended for marinating skinless chicken (12 hours with skin), and to really tenderize beef or lamb, 8 hours to overnight is ideal. Food should be refrigerated while marinating but brought back to room temperature before cooking to achieve optimum flavour.

Leftover marinades can be brushed over the food while it is cooking, or heated and served as a sauce, but make sure always to boil the marinade for at least 1 minute before serving.

Because many marinades have an acid-based ingredient, it is best to marinate food in shallow nonmetallic dishes. Heavy-duty plastic bags are also good for marinating foods.

Prepared marinades can be stored in screw-top jars in the refrigerator for up to two weeks.

Sweet Chilli Marinade
FOR 450 G/1 LB FISH, SEAFOOD OR CHICKEN

2 tbsp vegetable oil
2 tbsp Thai sweet chilli sauce
2 tbsp lemon or lime juice
3 cloves garlic, chopped
3 tsp grated ginger
1 tbsp freshly chopped coriander
salt and pepper to taste

Thai Lime Marinade
FOR 900 G/2 LB PRAWNS, BABY OCTOPUS OR FISH FILLETS

250 ml/8 fl oz coconut milk
50 ml/2 fl oz olive oil
50 ml/2 fl oz lime juice
2 tbsp finely grated lime zest
1 tbsp finely grated fresh ginger
2 cloves garlic, crushed
2 small red chilli peppers, thinly sliced
2 tbsp packed brown sugar
1 tbsp fish sauce

Soy and Basil Marinade
FOR 450 G/1 LB BEEF, LAMB OR PORK

2 tbsp vegetable oil
1 tbsp chopped basil leaves
3 tbsp soy sauce
grated rind of 1 lemon
3 cloves garlic, chopped
salt and pepper to taste

Ginger Marinade
FOR 450 G/1 LB VEGETABLES

2 tbsp vegetable oil
2 tsp sesame oil
2 cloves garlic, chopped
2 tsp grated ginger
salt and pepper to taste

Sweet and Sour Marinade
FOR 1.5 KG/3 LB PORK (SPARERIBS, LOIN OR CHOPS)

1 small pineapple, peeled, cut lengthwise into quarters, cored and thinly sliced (or 750 g/1½ lb tinned pineapple)

125 ml/4 fl oz pineapple juice
50 ml/2 fl oz lime juice
2 cloves crushed garlic
1 small red chilli pepper, finely chopped
60 g/2 oz packed brown sugar

Grapefruit and Brandy Marinade

FOR 1.1 KG/2¼ LB LAMB

125 ml/4 fl oz grapefruit juice
1 grapefruit, peeled, pith removed, cut into
    segments and seeded
75 g/3 oz honey
50 ml/2 fl oz brandy
50 ml/2 fl oz dry white wine
2 tbsp fresh thyme leaves
freshly ground pepper

Cranberry Marinade

FOR 900 G/2 LB POULTRY OR FISH

185 g/6½ oz cranberries
2 tbsp red wine vinegar
50 ml/2 fl oz olive oil
2 tbsp finely grated orange zest
2 cinnamon sticks
1 tbsp finely grated fresh ginger
3 tbsp packed brown sugar

Raspberry Marinade

FOR 700 G/1½ LB POULTRY OR FISH

225 g/8 oz raspberries
50 ml/2 fl oz raspberry vinegar
125 ml/4 fl oz olive oil
10 g/¼ oz fresh tarragon leaves
freshly ground pepper

1. Place the marinade ingredients in a screw-top jar or jug and mix well.

2. Place the fish, chicken, meat or vegetables into a shallow non metallic dish.

3. Pour or brush the marinade over the food. Cover and refrigerate.

4. Drain, then cook on the heated barbecue or grill, basting regularly with leftover marinade

Essential Hygiene in the Kitchen

It is well worth remembering that many foods can carry some form of bacteria. In most cases, the worst it will lead to is a bout of food poisoning or gastroenteritis, although for certain groups this can be more serious. The risk can be reduced or eliminated by good food hygiene and proper cooking.

Do not buy food that is past its sell-by date and do not consume any food that is past its use-by date. When buying food, use the eyes and nose. If the food looks tired, limp or a bad colour or it has a rank, acrid or simply bad smell, do not buy or eat it under any circumstances.

Regularly clean, defrost and clear out the refrigerator or freezer – it is worth checking the packaging to see exactly how long each product is safe to freeze.

Dish cloths and tea towels must be washed and changed regularly. Ideally use disposable cloths which should be replaced on a daily basis. More durable cloths should be

left to soak in bleach, then washed in the washing machine on a boil wash.

Always keep your hands, cooking utensils and food preparation surfaces clean and never allow pets to climb on to any work surfaces.

Buying

Avoid bulk buying where possible, especially fresh produce such as meat, poultry, fish, fruit and vegetables unless buying for the freezer. Fresh foods lose their nutritional value rapidly so buying a little at a time minimises loss of nutrients. It also eliminates a packed refrigerator which reduces the effectiveness of the refrigeration process.

When buying frozen foods, ensure that they are not heavily iced on the outside. Place in the freezer as soon as possible after purchase.

Preparation

Make sure that all work surfaces and utensils are clean and dry. Separate chopping boards should be used for raw and cooked meats, fish and vegetables. It is worth washing all fruits and vegetables regardless of whether they are going to be eaten raw or lightly cooked. Do not reheat food more than once.

All poultry must be thoroughly thawed before cooking. Leave the food in the refrigerator until it is completely thawed. Once defrosted, the chicken should be cooked as soon as possible. The only time food can be refrozen is when the food has been thoroughly thawed then cooked. Once the food has cooled then it can be frozen again for one month.

All poultry and game (except for duck) must be cooked thoroughly. When cooked the juices will run clear. Other meats, like minced meat and pork should be cooked right the way through. Fish should turn opaque, be firm in texture and break easily into large flakes.

Storing, Refrigerating and Freezing

Meat, poultry, fish, seafood and dairy products should all be refrigerated. The temperature of the refrigerator should be between 1–5°C/34–41°F while the freezer temperature should not rise above -18°C/-0.4°F. When refrigerating cooked food, allow it to cool down completely before refrigerating. Hot food will raise the temperature of the refrigerator and possibly affect or spoil other food stored in it.

Food within the refrigerator and freezer should always be covered. Raw and cooked food should be stored in separate parts of the refrigerator. Cooked food should be kept on the top shelves of the refrigerator, while raw meat, poultry and fish should be placed on bottom shelves to avoid drips and cross-contamination.

High-Risk Foods

Certain foods may carry risks to people who are considered vulnerable such as the elderly, the ill, pregnant women, babies and those suffering from a recurring illness. It is advisable to avoid those foods which belong to a higher-risk category.

There is a slight chance that some eggs carry the bacteria salmonella. Cook the eggs until both the yolk and the white are firm to eliminate this risk. Sauces including Hollandaise, mayonnaise, mousses, soufflés and meringues all use raw or lightly cooked eggs, as do custard-based dishes, ice creams and sorbets. These are all considered high-risk foods to the vulnerable groups mentioned above. Certain meats and poultry also carry the potential risk of salmonella and so should be cooked thoroughly until the juices run clear and there is no pinkness left. Unpasteurised products such as milk, cheese (especially soft cheese), pâté, meat (both raw and cooked) all have the potential risk of listeria and should be avoided.

When buying seafood, buy from a reputable source. Fish should have bright clear eyes, shiny skin and bright pink or red gills. The fish should feel stiff to the touch, with a slight smell of sea air and iodine. The flesh of fish steaks and fillets should be translucent with no signs of discolouration. Avoid any molluscs that are open or do not close when tapped lightly. Univalves such as cockles or winkles should withdraw into their shells when lightly prodded. Squid and octopus should have firm flesh and a pleasant sea smell.

Care is required when freezing seafood. It is imperative to check whether the fish has been frozen before. If it has been, then it should not be frozen again under any circumstances.

Nutrition
The Role of Essential Nutrients

A healthy and well-balanced diet is the body's primary energy source. In children, it constitutes the building blocks for future health as well as providing lots of energy. In adults, it encourages self-healing and regeneration within the body. A well-balanced diet will provide the body with all the essential nutrients it needs. This can be achieved by eating a variety of foods, demonstrated in the pyramid below:

Fats
milk, yoghurt
and cheese

Proteins
meat, fish, poultry, eggs,
nuts and pulses

*Fruits and
Vegetables*

Starchy Carbohydrates
cereals, potatoes, bread, rice and pasta

Fats

Fats fall into two categories: saturated and unsaturated fats. It is very important that a healthy balance is achieved within the diet. Fats are an essential part of the diet and a source of energy and provide essential fatty acids and fat soluble vitamins. The right balance of fats should boost the body's immunity to infection and keep muscles, nerves and arteries in good condition. Saturated fats are of animal origin and are hard when stored at room temperature. They can be found in dairy produce, meat, eggs, margarines and hard white cooking fat (lard) as well as in manufactured products such as pies, biscuits and cakes. A high intake of saturated fat over many years has been proven to increase heart disease and high blood cholesterol levels and often leads to weight gain. The aim of a healthy diet is to keep the fat content low in the foods that we eat. Lowering the amount of saturated fat that we consume is very important, but this does not mean that it is good to consume lots of other types of fat.

There are two kinds of unsaturated fats: poly-unsaturated fats and monounsaturated fats. Poly-unsaturated fats include the following oils: safflower oil, soybean oil, corn oil and sesame oil. Within the poly-unsaturated group are Omega oils. The Omega-3 oils are of significant interest because they have been found to be particularly beneficial to coronary health and can encourage brain growth and development. Omega-3 oils are derived from oily fish such as salmon, mackerel, herring, pilchards and sardines. It is recommended that we should eat these types of fish at least once a week. However, for those who do not eat fish or who are vegetarians, liver oil supplements are available in most supermarkets and health shops. It is suggested that these supplements should be taken on a daily basis. The most popular oils that are high in monounsaturates are olive oil, sunflower oil and peanut oil. The Mediterranean diet, which is based on a diet high in mono-unsaturated fats, is recommended for heart health. Also, monounsaturated fats are known to help reduce the levels of LDL (the bad) cholestrol.

Proteins

Composed of amino acids (proteins' building bricks), proteins perform a wide variety of essential functions for the body including supplying energy and building and repairing tissues. Good sources of proteins are eggs, milk, yoghurt, cheese, meat, fish, poultry, eggs, nuts and pulses. (See the second level of the pyramid.) Some of these foods, however, contain saturated fats. To strike a nutritional balance eat generous amounts of vegetable protein foods such as soya, beans, lentils, peas and nuts.

Fruits and Vegetables

Not only are fruits and vegetables the most visually appealing foods, but they are extremely good for us, providing essential vitamins and minerals essential for growth, repair and protection in the human body. Fruits and vegetables are low in calories and are responsible for regulating the body's metabolic processes and controlling the composition of its fluids and cells.

Minerals

CALCIUM Important for healthy bones and teeth, nerve transmission, muscle contraction, blood clotting and hormone function. Calcium promotes a healthy heart, improves skin, relieves aching muscles and bones, maintains the correct acid-alkaline balance and reduces menstrual cramps. Good sources are dairy products, small bones of small fish, nuts, pulses, fortified white flours, breads and green leafy vegetables.

CHROMIUM Part of the glucose tolerance factor, chromium balances blood sugar levels, helps to normalise hunger and reduce cravings, improves lifespan, helps protect DNA and is essential for heart function. Good sources are brewer's yeast, wholemeal bread, rye bread, oysters, potatoes, green peppers, butter and parsnips.

IODINE Important for the manufacture of thyroid hormones and for normal development. Good sources of iodine are seafood, seaweed, milk and dairy products.

IRON As a component of haemoglobin, iron carries oxygen around the body. It is vital for normal growth and development. Good sources are liver, corned beef, red meat, fortified breakfast cereals, pulses, green leafy vegetables, egg yolk and cocoa and cocoa products.

MAGNESIUM Important for efficient functioning of metabolic enzymes and development of the skeleton. Magnesium promotes healthy muscles by helping them to relax and is therefore good for PMS. It is also important for heart muscles and the nervous system. Good sources are nuts, green vegetables, meat, cereals, milk and yoghurt.

PHOSPHORUS Forms and maintains bones and teeth, builds muscle tissue, helps maintain the body's pH and aids metabolism and energy production. Phosphorus is present in almost all foods.

POTASSIUM Enables nutrients to move into cells, while waste products move out; promotes healthy nerves and muscles; maintains fluid balance in the body; helps secretion of insulin for blood sugar control to produce constant energy; relaxes muscles; maintains heart functioning and stimulates gut movement to encourage proper elimination. Good sources are fruit, vegetables, milk and bread.

SELENIUM Antioxidant properties help to protect against free radicals and carcinogens. Selenium reduces inflammation, stimulates the immune system to fight infections, promotes a healthy heart and helps vitamin E's action. It is also required for the male reproductive system and is needed for metabolism. Good sources are tuna, liver, kidney, meat, eggs, cereals, nuts and dairy products.

SODIUM Important in helping to control body fluid and balance, preventing dehydration. Sodium is involved in muscle and nerve function and helps move nutrients into cells. All foods are good sources, however processed, pickled and salted foods are richest in sodium.

ZINC Important for metabolism and the healing of wounds. It also aids ability to cope with stress, promotes a healthy nervous system and brain especially in the growing foetus, aids bones and teeth formation and is essential for constant energy. Good sources are liver, meat, pulses, whole-grain cereals, nuts and oysters.

Vitamins

VITAMIN A Important for cell growth and development and for the formation of visual pigments in the eye. Vitamin A comes in two forms: retinol and beta-carotenes. Retinol is found in liver, meat and meat products and whole milk and its products. Beta-carotene is a powerful antioxidant and is found in red and yellow fruits and vegetables such as carrots, mangoes and apricots.

VITAMIN B1 Important in releasing energy from carboydrate-containing foods. Good sources are yeast and yeast products, bread, fortified breakfast cereals and potatoes.

VITAMIN B2 Important for metabolism of proteins, fats and carbohydrates to produce energy. Good sources are meat, yeast extracts, fortified breakfast cereals and milk and its products.

VITAMIN B3 Required for the metabolism of food into energy production. Good sources are milk and milk products, fortified breakfast cereals, pulses, meat, poultry and eggs.

VITAMIN B5 Important for the metabolism of food and energy production. All foods are good sources but especially fortified breakfast cereals, whole-grain bread and dairy products.

VITAMIN B6 Important for metabolism of protein and fat. Vitamin B6 may also be involved with the regulation of sex hormones. Good sources are liver, fish, pork, soya beans and peanuts.

VITAMIN B12 Important for the production of red blood cells and DNA. It is vital for growth and the nervous system. Good sources are meat, fish, eggs, poultry and milk.

BIOTIN Important for metabolism of fatty acids. Good sources of biotin are liver, kidney, eggs and nuts. Micro-organisms also manufacture this vitamin in the gut.

VITAMIN C Important for healing wounds and the formation of collagen which keeps skin and bones strong. It is an important antioxidant. Good sources are fruits, soft summer fruits and vegetables.

VITAMIN D Important for absorption and handling of calcium to help build bone strength. Good sources are oily fish, eggs, whole milk and milk products, margarine and of course sufficient exposure to sunlight, as vitamin D is made in the skin.

VITAMIN E Important as an antioxidant vitamin helping to protect cell membranes from damage. Good sources are vegetable oils, margarines, seeds, nuts and green vegetables.

FOLIC ACID Critical during pregnancy for the development of the brain and nerves. It is always essential for brain and nerve function and is needed for utilising protein and red blood cell formation. Good sources are whole-grain cereals, fortified breakfast cereals, green leafy vegetables, oranges and liver.

VITAMIN K Important for controlling blood clotting. Good sources are cauliflower, Brussels sprouts, lettuce, cabbage, beans, broccoli, peas, asparagus, potatoes, corn oil, tomatoes and milk.

Carbohydrates

Carbohydrates are an energy source and come in two forms: starch and sugar carbohydrates. Starch carbohydrates are also known as complex carbohydrates and they include all cereals, potatoes, breads, rice and pasta. (See the fourth level of the pyramid). Eating whole-grain varieties of these foods also provides fibre. Diets high in fibre are believed to be beneficial in helping to prevent bowel cancer and can also keep cholesterol down. High-fibre diets are also good for those concerned about weight gain. Fibre is bulky so fills the stomach, therefore reducing hunger pangs. Sugar carbohydrates, which are also known as fast-release carbohydrates (because of the quick fix of energy they give to the body), include sugar and sugar-sweetened products such as jams and syrups. Milk provides lactose, which is a milk sugar, and fruits provide fructose, which is a fruit sugar.

Fish & Seafood

Gingered Cod Steaks

SERVES 4

2.5 cm/1 inch piece fresh
   root ginger, peeled
4 spring onions
2 tsp freshly chopped

parsley
1 tbsp soft brown sugar
4 x 175 g/6 oz thick cod steaks
salt and freshly ground

black pepper
25 g/1 oz butter
salad or freshly cooked
   vegetables, to serve

Prepare the barbecue, or preheat the grill and line the grill rack with a layer of tinfoil. Coarsely grate the piece of ginger. Trim the spring onions and cut into thin strips.

Mix the spring onions, ginger, chopped parsley and sugar. Add 1 tablespoon of water.

Wipe the fish steaks. Season to taste with salt and pepper. Place on to 4 separate 20.5 x 20.5 cm/8 x 8 inch kitchen foil squares.

Carefully spoon the spring onions and ginger mixture over the fish. Cut the butter into small cubes and place over the fish.

Loosely fold the foil over the steaks to enclose the fish and to make a parcel. Place on the barbecue or under the preheated grill and cook for 10–15 minutes or until cooked and the flesh has turned opaque.

Place the fish parcels on individual serving plates. Serve immediately with the salad or freshly cooked vegetables.

Try This: FOR AN ALTERNATIVE: 28   FOR A MEAT OR POULTRY OPTION: 70

Cod with
Fennel & Cardamom

SERVES 4

1 garlic clove, peeled
    and crushed
finely grated rind of 1 lemon
1 tsp lemon juice

1 tbsp olive oil
1 fennel bulb
1 tbsp cardamom pods
salt and freshly ground

black pepper
4 x 175 g/6 oz thick
    cod fillets

Prepare the barbecue or preheat the oven to 190°C/375°F/Gas Mark 5. Place the garlic in a small bowl with the lemon rind, juice and olive oil and stir well. Cover and leave to infuse for at least 30 minutes. Stir well before using.

Trim the fennel bulb, thinly slice and place in a bowl.

Place the cardamom pods in a pestle and mortar and lightly pound to crack the pods. Alternatively place in a polythene bag and pound gently with a rolling pin. Add the crushed cardamom to the fennel slices.

Season the fish with salt and pepper and place on to 4 separate 20.5 x 20.5 cm/8 x 8 inch parchment paper squares.

Spoon the fennel mixture over the fish and drizzle with the infused oil. If cooking on the barbecue, place the parcels on squares of kitchen foil and fold up around the paper for protection; place on the barbecue. If cooking on the oven, place the paper parcels on a baking sheet and put into the preheated oven. Cook on the barbecue for 12–15 minutes, or in the oven for 8–10 minutes, or until cooked. Serve immediately in the paper parcels.

Try This: FOR AN ALTERNATIVE: 26 FOR A MEAT OR POULTRY OPTION: 74

Barbecued Fish Kebabs

SERVES 4

at least 4 wooden skewers
450 g/1 lb herring or mackerel
   fillets, cut into chunks
2 small red onions, peeled
   and quartered
16 cherry tomatoes

salt and freshly ground
   black pepper
salad or couscous, to serve

For the sauce:
150 ml/¼ pint fish stock

5 tbsp tomato ketchup
2 tbsp Worcestershire sauce
2 tbsp wine vinegar
2 tbsp brown sugar
2 drops Tabasco
2 tbsp tomato purée

Soak the skewers in cold water for 30 minutes to prevent them from catching alight during cooking, then drain.

Meanwhile, prepare the barbecue. Or, if using a grill, line the rack with a single layer of kitchen foil and, 2 minutes before use, preheat the grill at a high temperature.

Meanwhile, prepare the sauce. Add the fish stock, tomato ketchup, Worcestershire sauce, vinegar, sugar, Tabasco and tomato purée to a small saucepan. Stir well and leave to simmer for 5 minutes.

When ready to cook, drain the skewers, if necessary, then thread the fish chunks, the quartered red onions and the cherry tomatoes alternately on to the skewers.

Season the kebabs to taste with salt and pepper and brush with the sauce. Cook on the barbecue or under the preheated grill for 8–10 minutes, basting with the sauce occasionally during cooking. Turn the kebabs often to ensure that they are cooked thoroughly and evenly on all sides. Serve immediately with salad or couscous.

Try This: FOR AN ALTERNATIVE: 38   FOR A MEAT OR POULTRY OPTION: 88

Barbecued Salmon with Wasabi Butter

SERVES 4

125 g/4 oz butter, softened
2 tsp wasabi paste
grated rind of 1 lime
1 tbsp lime juice
½ tsp freshly ground

black pepper
4 salmon steaks, approx.
6 oz/175 g each
2 tbsp vegetable oil
fresh coriander, to garnish

For crispy fried potatoes:
3 potatoes, peeled and very
thinly sliced
125 ml/4 fl oz vegetable oil,
for frying

Prepare the barbecue. Using a sharp knife, cut the bone away from each salmon steak to create fillets. Repeat with the remaining salmon steaks. Remove the skin.

In a mixing bowl, beat the butter until soft. Add the wasabi paste, rind, juice and pepper and mix until well combined. Refrigerate until firm. Brush the salmon with oil. On the barbecue or in a grill pan, cook the salmon 2–3 minutes each side (the salmon should remain pink in the centre), then allow to stand 5 minutes.

Place onto serving plates. Using a teaspoon or melon baller, scoop the wasabi butter onto the salmon pieces. Serve with crispy fried potatoes and garnish with fresh coriander.

To make crispy fried potatoes, pat the potato dry with kitchen towel. On a barbecue tray or In a frying pan, heat oil over medium heat and, working in batches, fry the potato slices for about 2 minutes, or until golden and crisp. Remove with a slotted spoon and drain on kitchen towel.

Try This: FOR AN ALTERNATIVE: 48 FOR A MEAT OR POULTRY OPTION: 90

Seared Tuna with Pernod & Thyme

SERVES 4

4 tuna or swordfish steaks
salt and freshly ground
   black pepper
3 tbsp Pernod

1 tbsp olive oil
zest and juice of 1 lime
2 tsp fresh thyme leaves
4 sun-dried tomatoes

To serve:
freshly cooked mixed
   rice (optional)
tossed green salad

Wipe the fish steaks with a damp cloth or dampened kitchen paper.

Season both sides of the fish to taste with salt and pepper, then place in a shallow bowl and reserve.

Mix together the Pernod, olive oil, lime zest and juice with the fresh thyme leaves. Finely chop the sun-dried tomatoes and add to the Pernod mixture.

Pour the Pernod mixture over the fish and chill in the refrigerator for about 2 hours, spooning the marinade occasionally over the fish.

Meanwhile prepare the barbecue, or when ready to cook, heat a griddle or heavy-based frying pan. Drain the fish, reserving the marinade. Cook the fish for 3–4 minutes on each side for a steak that is still slightly pink in the middle. Or, if liked, cook the fish for 1–2 minutes longer on each side if you prefer your fish cooked through. If you want to avoid the marinade elements dropping through the barbecue rack, you could try using a griddle plate or barbecue tray over the barbecue. If doing this remember that the tuna will take at least twice as long than if being cooked straight on the barbecue.

Place the remaining marinade in a small saucepan and bring to the boil. Pour the marinade over the fish and serve immediately, with the mixed rice, if using, and salad.

Try This: FOR AN ALTERNATIVE: 36   FOR A MEAT OR POULTRY OPTION: 68

Seared Tuna
with Italian Salsa

SERVES 4

4 x 175 g/6 oz tuna or
    swordfish steaks
salt and freshly ground
    black pepper
3 tbsp Pernod
2 tbsp olive oil
zest and juice of 1 lemon
2 tsp fresh thyme leaves
2 tsp fennel seeds, lightly
    roasted

4 sun-dried tomatoes,
    chopped
1 tsp dried chilli flakes
assorted salad leaves,
    to serve

For the salsa:
1 white onion, peeled and
    finely chopped
2 tomatoes, deseeded

and sliced
2 tbsp freshly shredded
    basil leaves
1 red chilli, deseeded and
    finely sliced
3 tbsp extra-virgin olive oil
2 tsp balsamic vinegar
1 tsp caster sugar

Wipe the fish and season lightly with salt and pepper, then place in a shallow dish. Mix together the Pernod, olive oil, lemon zest and juice, thyme, fennel seeds, sun-dried tomatoes and chilli flakes and pour over the fish. Cover lightly and leave to marinate in a cool place for 1–2 hours, occasionally spooning the marinade over the fish.

Meanwhile, prepare the barbecue. Mix all the salsa ingredients together in a small bowl. Season to taste with salt and pepper, then cover and leave for about 30 minutes to marinate.

If not using the barbecue, when ready to cook, lightly oil a griddle pan and heat until very hot. Drain the fish, reserving the marinade. Cook the fish for 3–4 minutes on each side, taking care not to overcook them – the tuna steaks should be a little pink inside. If you want to avoid the marinade elements dropping through the barbecue rack, you could try using a griddle plate or barbecue tray on the barbecue. Remember that the tuna will take at least twice as long as if being cooked straight on the barbecue.

Pour any remaining marinade into a small saucepan, bring to the boil and boil for 1 minute. Serve the steaks hot with the marinade, chilled salsa and a few assorted salad leaves.

Try This: FOR AN ALTERNATIVE: 34 FOR A MEAT OR POULTRY OPTION: 84

Citrus Monkfish Kebabs

SERVES 4

For the marinade:
1 tbsp sunflower oil
finely grated rind and juice
  of 1 lime
1 tbsp lemon juice
1 sprig freshly chopped
  rosemary

1 tbsp whole-grain mustard
1 garlic clove, peeled
  and crushed
salt and freshly ground
  black pepper

For the kebabs:
8 wooden skewers
450 g/1 lb monkfish tail
8 raw tiger prawns
1 small green courgette,
  trimmed and sliced
4 tbsp of crème fraîche

Prepare the barbecue, or line the grill rack with foil and preheat the grill 2 minutes before using. Mix all the marinade ingredients together in a small bowl and reserve.

Using a sharp knife, cut down both sides of the monkfish tail. Remove the bone and discard. Cut away and discard any skin, then cut the monkfish into bite-sized cubes.

Peel the prawns, leaving the tails intact and remove the thin black vein that runs down the back of each prawn. Place the fish and prawns in a shallow dish.

Pour the marinade, reserving 2 tablespoons, over the fish and prawns. Cover lightly and leave to marinate in the refrigerator for 30 minutes. Spoon the marinade over the fish and prawns occasionally during this time. Soak the skewers in cold water for 30 minutes, then drain.

Thread the cubes of fish, prawns and courgettes on to the drained skewers. Place on the barbecue or arrange on the grill rack then place under the preheated grill, and cook for 5–7 minutes, or until cooked thoroughly and the prawns have turned pink. Occasionally brush with the remaining marinade and turn the kebabs during cooking.

Mix the reserved marinade with the crème fraîche and serve as a dip with the kebabs.

Try This: FOR AN ALTERNATIVE: 54   FOR A MEAT OR POULTRY OPTION: 88

Prawn, Lime & Chilli Pepper Skewers

SERVES 3–4

12 king prawns
4 tbsp vegetable oil
freshly ground black pepper
3 tbsp lime juice
2 tsp grated ginger

2 cloves garlic, finely
    chopped
12 bamboo skewers
2 limes, cut into 6
    wedges each

12 small red chilli peppers
2 red onions, cut into 6
    wedges each
40 g/1½ oz mixed salad
    greens, for serving

Peel the prawns, leaving the tails on. Using a sharp knife, remove the black vein along the back of the prawns. Place the prawns in a shallow nonmetallic dish.

In a small bowl, combine 2 tablespoons of the oil, some black pepper, the lime juice, ginger, and garlic, mix well and pour over the prawns. Cover the dish with clingfilm and refrigerate for 1 hour.

Meanwhile, prepare the barbecue or line the grill rack with foil and preheat the grill 2 minutes before using. Soak the bamboo skewers in cold water for 30 minutes, then drain.

Remove the prawns from the marinade. Thread a prawn, lime wedge, chilli pepper and red onion wedge onto each skewer. Away from the hot coals, brush the barbecue grill (or the grill rack) with the remaining oil. Cook the skewers for 2–3 minutes on each side, or until the prawns change colour. Remove from the grill and serve warm with salad greens.

Try This: FOR AN ALTERNATIVE: 56   FOR A MEAT OR POULTRY OPTION: 76

Sardines with Redcurrants

SERVES 4

2 tbsp redcurrant jelly
finely grated rind of 1 lime
2 tbsp medium dry sherry
450 g /1 lb fresh sardines,
   cleaned, and heads

removed if preferred
sea salt and freshly ground
   black pepper
lime wedges, to garnish

To serve:
fresh redcurrants
fresh green salad

Prepare the barbecue, or preheat the grill and line the grill rack with kitchen foil 2–3 minutes before cooking.

Warm the redcurrant jelly in a bowl standing over a pan of gently simmering water and stir until smooth. Add the lime rind and sherry to the bowl and stir well until blended.

Lightly rinse the sardines and pat dry with absorbent kitchen paper.

Place on a chopping board and with a sharp knife make several diagonal cuts across the flesh of each fish. Season the sardines inside the cavities with salt and pepper.

Gently brush the warm marinade over the skin and inside the cavities of the sardines. Place on the barbecue, or on the grill rack under the preheated grill, and cook for 8–10 minutes, or until the fish are cooked.

Carefully turn the sardines over at least once during grilling. Baste occasionally with the remaining redcurrant and lime marinade. Garnish with the redcurrants. Serve immediately with the salad and lime wedges.

Try This: FOR AN ALTERNATIVE: 44   FOR A MEAT OR POULTRY OPTION: 66

Sardines in Vine Leaves

SERVES 4

8–16 vine leaves in brine,
    drained
2 spring onions
6 tbsp olive oil
2 tbsp lime juice
2 tbsp freshly chopped
    oregano

1 tsp mustard powder
salt and freshly ground
    black pepper
8 sardines, cleaned
8 bay leaves
8 sprigs of fresh dill

To garnish:
lime wedges
sprigs of fresh dill

To serve:
olive salad
crusty bread

Prepare the barbecue, or preheat the grill and line the grill rack with kitchen foil just before cooking. Cut 8 pieces of string about 25.5 cm/10 inches long, and leave to soak in cold water for about 10 minutes. Cover the vine leaves in almost boiling water. Leave for 20 minutes, then drain and rinse thoroughly. Pat the vine leaves dry with absorbent kitchen paper.

Trim the spring onions and finely chop, then place into a small bowl. With a balloon whisk beat in the olive oil, lime juice, oregano, mustard powder and season to taste with salt and pepper. Cover with clingfilm and leave in the refrigerator, until required. Stir the mixture before using.

Prepare the sardines, by making 2 slashes on both sides of each fish and brush with a little of the lime juice mixture. Place a bay leaf and a dill sprig inside each sardine cavity and wrap with 1–2 vine leaves, depending on size. Brush with the lime mixture and tie the vine leaves in place with string.

Cook the fish on the barbecue, or under a medium hot grill, for 4–5 minutes on each side, brushing with a little more of the lime mixture if necessary. Leave the fish to rest, unwrap and discard the vine leaves. Garnish with lime wedges and sprigs of fresh dill and serve with the remaining lime mixture, olive salad and crusty bread.

Try This: FOR AN ALTERNATIVE: 42 FOR A MEAT OR POULTRY OPTION: 102

Red Mullet with Orange & Anchovy Sauce

SERVES 4

2 oranges
4 x 175 g/6 oz red mullet,
   cleaned and descaled
salt and freshly ground
   black pepper
4 sprigs of fresh rosemary

1 lemon, sliced
2 tbsp olive oil
2 garlic cloves, peeled
   and crushed
6 anchovy fillets in oil,
   drained and roughly

chopped
2 tsp freshly chopped
   rosemary
1 tsp lemon juice

Prepare the barbecue, or preheat the grill and line the grill rack with kitchen foil just before cooking. Peel the oranges with a sharp knife, over a bowl in order to catch the juice. Cut into thin slices and reserve. If necessary, make up the juice to 150 ml/¼ pint with extra juice.

Place the fish on a chopping board and make 2 diagonal slashes across the thickest part of both sides of the fish. Season well, both inside and out, with salt and pepper. Tuck a rosemary sprig and a few lemon slices inside the cavity of each fish. Brush the fish with a little of the olive oil and then cook on the barbecue or under the preheated grill for 4–5 minutes on each side. The flesh should just fall away from the bone.

Heat the remaining oil in a saucepan and gently fry the garlic and anchovies for 3–4 minutes. Do not allow to brown. Add the chopped rosemary and plenty of black pepper. The anchovies will be salty enough, so do not add any salt. Stir in the orange slices with their juice and the lemon juice. Simmer gently until heated through. Spoon the sauce over the red mullet and serve immediately.

Try This: FOR AN ALTERNATIVE: 32 FOR A MEAT OR POULTRY OPTION: 106

Salmon Fish Cakes

SERVES 4

225 g/8 oz potatoes, peeled
450 g/1 lb salmon
   fillet, skinned
125 g/4 oz carrot, trimmed
   and peeled
2 tbsp grated lemon rind

2–3 tbsp freshly
   chopped coriander
1 medium egg yolk
salt and freshly ground
   black pepper
2 tbsp plain white flour

few fine sprays of oil

To serve:
prepared tomato sauce
tossed green salad
crusty bread

Prepare the barbecue. Cube the potatoes and cook in lightly salted boiling water for 15 minutes. Drain and mash the potatoes. Place in a mixing bowl and reserve.

Place the salmon in a food processor and blend to form a chunky purée. Add the purée to the potatoes and mix together.

Coarsely grate the carrot and add to the fish with the lemon rind and the coriander.

Add the egg yolk, season to taste with salt and pepper, then gently mix the ingredients together. With damp hands form the mixture into 4 large fish cakes. Coat in the flour and place on a plate. Cover loosely and chill for at least 30 minutes.

When ready to cook, place the fish cakes onto a hot, oiled griddle plate on the barbecue, or in a griddle pan on the hob. Cook on both sides for 3–4 minutes or until the fish is cooked. Add an extra spray of oil if needed during the cooking, but be careful not to let any oil drop onto the hot coals or it will catch alight.

When the fish cakes are cooked, serve immediately with the tomato sauce, green salad and crusty bread.

Try This: FOR AN ALTERNATIVE: 50   FOR A MEAT OR POULTRY OPTION: 100

Tuna Fish Burgers

MAKES 8

450 g/1 lb potatoes, peeled
   and cut into chunks
50 g/2 oz butter
2 tbsp milk
400 g can tuna in oil
1 spring onion, trimmed and
   finely chopped

1 tbsp freshly chopped parsley
salt and freshly ground
   black pepper
2 medium eggs, beaten
2 tbsp seasoned plain flour
125 g/4 oz fresh white
   breadcrumbs

4 tbsp vegetable oil

To serve:
4 sesame seed baps
fat chips (optional)
mixed salad
tomato chutney

Place the potatoes in a large saucepan, cover with boiling water and simmer until soft. Drain, then mash with 40 g/1½ oz of the butter and the milk. Turn into a large bowl. Drain the tuna, discarding the oil and flake into the bowl of potato. Stir well to mix.

Add the spring onions and parsley to the mixture and season to taste with salt and pepper. Add 1 tablespoon of the beaten egg to bind the mixture together. Chill in the refrigerator for at least 1 hour. Meanwhile, prepare the barbecue.

Shape the chilled mixture with your hands into 4 large burgers. First, coat the burgers with seasoned flour, then brush them with the remaining beaten egg, allowing any excess to drip back into the bowl. Finally, coat them evenly in the breadcrumbs, pressing the crumbs on with your hands, if necessary.

Place the burgers either directly onto the barbecue or onto a barbecue tray on top – either way, use a little of the oil to avoid sticking. Or, heat a little of the oil in a frying pan and fry the burgers. Cook for 2–3 minutes on each side until golden, adding more oil if necessary. Drain on absorbent kitchen paper, if necessary, and serve hot in baps, with chips, if using, mixed salad and chutney.

Try This: FOR AN ALTERNATIVE: 36   FOR A MEAT OR POULTRY OPTION: 78

Hot Tiger Prawns with Parma Ham

SERVES 4

½ cucumber, peeled if preferred
4 ripe tomatoes
12 raw tiger prawns
6 tbsp olive oil

4 garlic cloves, peeled and crushed
4 tbsp freshly chopped parsley
salt and freshly ground black pepper

6 slices of Parma ham, cut in half
4 slices flat Italian bread
4 tbsp dry white wine

If using the barbecue, soak some thin wooden skewers for 30 minutes before cooking.

Prepare the barbecue, or preheat the oven to 180°C/350°F/Gas Mark 4. Slice the cucumber and tomatoes thinly, then arrange on 4 large plates and reserve. Peel the prawns, leaving the tail shell intact and remove the thin black vein running down the back.

Whisk together 4 tablespoons of the olive oil, garlic and chopped parsley in a small bowl and season to taste with plenty of salt and pepper. Add the prawns to the mixture and stir until they are well coated. Remove the prawns, then wrap each one in a piece of Parma ham and, if cooking in the oven, secure each one with a cocktail stick. If using the barbecue, thread the wrapped prawns carefully onto the skewers so that they will sit on the barbecue more easily.

Place the prepared prawns on the barbecue, or on a lightly oiled baking sheet or dish in the preheated oven. Cook for 3 minutes on the barbecue, or 5 minutes in the oven, turning once. At the same time toast the slices of bread in the oven or on the barbecue.

Remove the prawns from the heat and spoon the wine over the prawns and bread. Return to the barbecue or oven and cook for a further 5 or 10 minutes respectively until piping hot.

Carefully remove the skewers or cocktail sticks and arrange 3 prawn rolls on each slice of bread. Place on top of the sliced cucumber and tomatoes and serve immediately.

Try This: FOR AN ALTERNATIVE: 40   FOR A MEAT OR POULTRY OPTION: 108

Scallops & Monkfish Kebabs with Fennel Sauce

SERVES 4

700 g/½lb monkfish tail
8 large fresh scallops
2 tbsp olive oil
1 garlic clove, peeled
    and crushed
freshly ground black pepper

1 fennel bulb, trimmed and
    thinly sliced
assorted salad leaves, to serve

For the sauce:
2 tbsp fennel seeds

pinch of chilli flakes
4 tbsp olive oil
2 tsp lemon juice
salt and freshly ground
    black pepper

Prepare the barbecue, and soak some wooden skewers. Place the monkfish on a chopping board and remove the skin and the bone that runs down the centre of the tail and discard. Lightly rinse and pat dry. Cut the 2 fillets into 12 equal-sized pieces and place in a shallow bowl. Remove the scallops from their shells, if necessary, and clean thoroughly discarding the black vein. Rinse lightly and pat dry. Put in the bowl with the fish.

Blend the 2 tablespoons of olive oil, the crushed garlic and a pinch of black pepper in a small bowl, then pour the mixture over the monkfish and scallops, making sure they are well coated. Cover lightly and leave to marinate in the refrigerator for at least 30 minutes, or longer if time permits. Spoon over the marinade occasionally.

Lightly crush the fennel seeds and chilli in a pestle and mortar. Stir in the 4 tablespoons of olive oil and lemon juice and season with salt and pepper. Cover and leave to infuse for 20 minutes.

Drain the monkfish and scallops, reserving the marinade and thread on to 4 skewers. Place on the hot barbecue or on a griddle pan coated with a fine spray of oil and heated until almost smoking, and cook for 5–6 minutes, turning halfway through and brushing with the marinade throughout. Brush the fennel slices with the fennel sauce and cook on the barbecue or griddle for 1 minute on each side. Serve the fennel, topped with the kebabs and drizzled with the fennel sauce. Serve with a few assorted salad leaves.

Try This: FOR AN ALTERNATIVE: 62   FOR A MEAT OR POULTRY OPTION: 96

Curried Prawn Kebabs

SERVES 4–6

1 tbsp vegetable oil
1 tsp fennel seeds
1 tsp cumin seeds
1 tsp turmeric
1 tsp chilli powder
1 tsp ground coriander

1 red chilli, deseeded and
   chopped
5 cm/2 inch piece fresh root
   ginger, peeled and grated
2 tbsp lime juice
300 ml/½ pint natural yogurt

350 g/12 oz raw large
   prawns, peeled
2–3 limes, cut into wedges
salad and Indian-style bread,
   to serve
4–8 wooden kebab skewers

Prepare the barbecue, or preheat the grill and line the grill rack with kitchen foil 2–3 minutes before cooking. Soak the skewers in cold water for at least 30 minutes, then drain.

Heat the oil in a wok or frying pan, add the seeds and fry for 30 seconds, or until they pop. Add the turmeric, chilli powder, ground coriander, chopped chilli and grated ginger and fry over a gentle heat for 2 minutes. Stir in the lime juice and cook, stirring, for 30 seconds. Remove from the heat and cool slightly before stirring in the yogurt.

Rinse the prawns and pat dry with absorbent kitchen paper, then place in a shallow dish large enough for the prawns to lie in a single layer. Pour the spicy yogurt over the prawns, cover lightly and leave to marinate in the refrigerator for at least 30 minutes, turning the prawns over a couple of times.

Drain the prawns, reserving the marinade, and thread them with the lime wedges onto the drained skewers. Cook on the barbecue for 4–5 minutes or under the grill for 6–8 minutes, or until cooked, turning the prawns over occasionally and brushing with a little of the reserved marinade. Move to the side of the barbecue or turn the heat down if the prawns are cooking too quickly and beginning to burn. Serve with salad and bread.

Try This: FOR AN ALTERNATIVE: 52   FOR A MEAT OR POULTRY OPTION: 98

Mixed Seafood Skewers

SERVES 4

12 bamboo skewers
225 g/8 oz king prawns
225 g/8 oz scallops, cleaned
350 g/12 oz white fish fillets,
    cut into 4-cm/1½-inch cubes
4 tbsp groundnut oil,

    divided in half
½ onion, coarsely chopped
2 cloves garlic
2 tsp grated ginger
2 stems lemongrass (white
    section only), chopped

1 tsp shrimp paste
4 tbsp soy sauce
1 tsp chilli oil
1 tsp sesame oil
25 g/1 oz mizuna leaves,
    to serve

Prepare the barbecue, or preheat the grill and line the grill rack with kitchen foil 2–3 minutes before cooking. Soak the bamboo skewers in cold water for 30 minutes, then drain.

Peel the prawns, leaving the tails on. Using a sharp knife, remove the black vein along the back of the prawns.

Pat the prawns, scallops and fish dry with kitchen towel and thread alternately onto the skewers. Brush the seafood skewers with 2 tablespoons of the groundnut oil, then place into a shallow nonmetallic dish.

In a food processor, combine the onion, garlic, ginger, lemongrass, shrimp paste, remaining groundnut oil, 1 tablespoon of the soy sauce, the chilli oil and sesame oil and process for about 30 seconds, until the mixture becomes a smooth paste.

Brush the seafood with the spice paste, then cover the dish with clingfilm and refrigerate for 30 minutes. On the barbecue or under the grill, cook the skewers for 3–4 minutes each side, or until the seafood changes colour. Remove from the grill. Serve warm with the remaining soy sauce as a dipping sauce and the mizuna leaves.

Try This: FOR AN ALTERNATIVE: 54   FOR A MEAT OR POULTRY OPTION: 82

Fish Steaks with Sake

SERVES 4

800 g/1¾ lb fish, or 4 fish
    steaks, approx. 200 g/7 oz
    each (choose any fish
    with firm, white flesh,
    such as monkfish, sea
    bass, grouper, halibut,

coley or cod)
2 tbsp vegetable oil
25 ml/1 fl oz sake
juice and grated rind of
    1 lime
2 tsp sea salt

1 tsp freshly ground
    black pepper
50 g/2 oz baby spinach
    leaves, to serve
2 tbsp additional grated lime
    rind, for serving

Prepare the barbecue, or preheat the grill and line the grill rack with kitchen foil 2–3 minutes before cooking. If using monkfish, cut down both sides of the monkfish tail using a sharp knife. Remove the bone and discard. Cut away and discard any skin if liked, then cut the monkfish into steaks.

In a bowl, combine the sake, lime juice and rind.

Sprinkle both sides of the fish steaks with salt and pepper. Away from the hot coals, lightly brush the grill rack with with oil. Cook the fish for 2–3 minutes on each side, or until it changes colour and flakes easily with a fork. Remove from the grill and brush each with the combined sake, juice and rind.

To serve, arrange the spinach leaves on serving plates and top with the fish steaks. Serve with extra lime rind.

Try This: FOR AN ALTERNATIVE: 32 FOR A MEAT OR POULTRY OPTION: 92

Monkfish with Vegetables

SERVES 4

300 g/10 oz parsnips, peeled
350 g/12 oz sweet potatoes, peeled
300 g/10 oz carrots, peeled
2 onions, peeled
4–6 garlic cloves, peeled

salt and freshly ground black pepper
2 tbsp olive oil
2 small monkfish tails, about 900 g/2 lb total weight, or 4 monkfish fillets, about

700 g/1½ lb total weight
2–3 sprigs of fresh rosemary
2 yellow peppers, deseeded
225 g/8 oz cherry tomatoes
2 tbsp freshly chopped parsley

Prepare a covered barbecue, or preheat the oven to 190°C/375°F/Gas Mark 5. Cut all the root vegetables, including the onions, into even-sized wedges and place in a large barbecue tray or roasting tin. Reserve 2 garlic cloves and add the remainder to the roasting tin. Season to taste with salt and pepper and pour over 1 tablespoon of the oil. Turn the vegetables over until lightly coated in the oil, then cook in the barbecue or oven for 20 minutes.

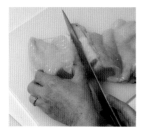

Meanwhile, cut the monkfish tails into fillets. Using a sharp knife, cut down both sides of the central bone to form 2 fillets from each tail. Discard any skin or membrane, then rinse thoroughly. Make small incisions down the length of the monkfish fillets.

Cut the reserved garlic cloves into small slivers and break the rosemary into small sprigs. Insert the garlic and rosemary into the incisions in the fish.

Cut the peppers into strips, then add to the tray together with the cherry tomatoes. Place the fish on top and drizzle with the remaining oil. Cook for a further 12–15 minutes, or until the vegetables and fish are thoroughly cooked. Serve sprinkled with chopped parsley.

Try This: FOR AN ALTERNATIVE: 38 FOR A MEAT OR POULTRY OPTION: 110

Jamaican Jerk Pork

ERVES 4

2 onions, peeled and chopped
2 garlic cloves, peeled
  and crushed
4 tbsp lime juice
2 tbsp each dark molasses,
  soy sauce and chopped
  fresh root ginger
2 jalapeño chillies, deseeded
  and chopped
½ tsp ground cinnamon

¼ tsp each ground allspice,
  ground nutmeg
4 pork loin chops, on the bone

For the rice:
175 g/6 oz dried red kidney
  beans, soaked overnight
1 tbsp vegetable oil
1 onion, peeled and
  finely chopped

1 celery stalk, trimmed
  and finely sliced
3 garlic cloves, peeled
  and crushed
2 bay leaves
225 g/8 oz long-grain white rice
475 ml/18 fl oz chicken
  or ham stock
sprigs of fresh flat-leaf
  parsley, to garnish

To make the jerk pork marinade, purée the onions, garlic, lime juice, molasses, soy sauce, ginger, chillies, cinnamon, allspice and nutmeg together in a food processor until smooth. Put the pork chops into a plastic or non-reactive dish and pour over the marinade, turning the chops to coat. Marinate in the refrigerator for at least 1 hour or overnight.

For the rice, drain the beans and place in a large saucepan with about 2 litres/3½ pints cold water. Bring to the boil and boil rapidly for 10 minutes. Reduce the heat, cover and simmer gently, for 1 hour until tender, adding more water if necessary. When cooked, drain well and mash roughly. Heat the oil for the rice in a saucepan with a tight-fitting lid and add the onion, celery and garlic. Cook gently for 5 minutes until softened. Add the bay leaves, rice and stock and stir. Bring to the boil, cover and cook very gently for 10 minutes. Add the beans and stir well again. Cook for a further 5 minutes, then remove from the heat. Meanwhille, prepare the barbecue.

When the barbecue is ready, or you have heated a griddle pan until almost smoking, remove the pork chops from the marinade, scraping off any surplus and add to the barbecue or pan. Cook for 5–8 minutes on each side, or until cooked. Garnish with the parsley and serve immediately with the rice, if using, or fresh salad.

Try This: FOR AN ALTERNATIVE: 68   FOR A FISH OR VEGETABLE OPTION: 126

Meat & Poultry

Jerked Steaks

SERVES 4–6

4 rump/sirloin steaks,
   125 g/4 oz each

For the jerk sauce:
1 tsp ground allspice
25 g/1 oz light muscovado
   sugar
1–2 garlic cloves, peeled and
   chopped
1 small red chilli, deseeded
   and chopped
few fresh thyme sprigs,
   leaves removed
1 tsp ground cinnamon

¼ tsp freshly grated nutmeg
salt and freshly ground
   black pepper
1 tbsp soy sauce

For the mango relish:
1 ripe mango, peeled,
   stoned and finely
   chopped
6 spring onions, trimmed
   and chopped
1–2 garlic cloves, peeled and
   crushed
1 red chilli, deseeded and

chopped
1 small, ripe but firm
   banana, peeled and
   chopped
1 tbsp lime juice
1 tbsp clear honey, warmed
50 g/2 oz unsweetened
   chopped dates
1 tsp ground cinnamon

To serve:
salad
potato wedges (optional)

Blend all the ingredients for the jerk sauce then rub over the steaks. Place on a plate, lightly cover and leave in the refrigerator for at least 30 minutes.

Mix together all the ingredients for the mango relish, cover and leave for 30 minutes to allow the flavours to develop.

Meanwhile, prepare the barbecue or, when ready to cook, heat a griddle pan or heavy-based frying pan until hot and a few drops of water sizzle when dropped into the pan. Add the steaks to the barbecue or pan and cook for 2–3 minutes on each side for rare, 3–4 minutes on each side for medium and 5–6 minutes on each side for well done.

Remove from the barbecue or pan and serve with the prepared relish, salad and potato wedges, if using.

Try This: FOR AN ALTERNATIVE: 66   FOR A FISH OR VEGETABLE OPTION: 26

Marinated Lamb Chops

SERVES 4

4 thick lamb chops
mixed salad or freshly cooked
   vegetables, to serve

For the marinade:
1 small bunch of fresh
   thyme, leaves removed

1 tbsp freshly
   chopped rosemary
1 tsp salt
2 garlic cloves, peeled
   and crushed
rind and juice of 1 lemon
2 tbsp olive oil

**For the garlic-fried
   potatoes:**
3 tbsp olive oil
550 g/1¼ lb potatoes,
   peeled and cut into
   1 cm/½ inch dice
6 unpeeled garlic cloves

Trim the chops of any excess fat, wipe with a clean damp cloth and reserve. To make the marinade, using a pestle and mortar, pound the thyme leaves and rosemary with the salt until pulpy. Add the garlic and continue pounding until crushed. Stir in the lemon rind and juice and the olive oil.

Pour the marinade over the lamb chops, turning them until they are well coated. Cover lightly and leave to marinate in the refrigerator for about 1 hour. Meanwhile, prepare the barbecue.

To make the potatoes, heat the oil in a large barbecue tray or non-stick frying pan. Add the potatoes and garlic and cook over a low heat for about 20 minutes, stirring occasionally. Increase the heat and cook for a further 10–15 minutes until golden. Drain on absorbent kitchen paper and add salt to taste. Keep warm.

Add the lamb chops to the barbecue or a hot griddle pan and cook for 3–4 minutes on each side until golden, but still pink in the middle. Serve with the potatoes and either a mixed salad or freshly cooked vegetables.

Try This: FOR AN ALTERNATIVE: 96   FOR A FISH OR VEGETABLE OPTION: 114

Grilled Steaks and Tomatoes

SERVES 4

For the saffron potatoes (optional):
700 g/1½ lb new potatoes, halved
few strands of saffron
300 ml/½ pint vegetable or beef stock
1 small onion, peeled and finely chopped

25 g/1 oz butter
salt and freshly ground black pepper

For the tomatoes:
2 tsp balsamic vinegar
2 tbsp olive oil
1 tsp caster sugar
salt and freshly ground

black pepper
8 plum tomatoes, halved

50 g/2 oz butter (if using a pan)
4 boneless sirloin steaks, each weighing 225 g/8 oz
2 tbsp freshly chopped parsley

Prepare the barbecue. If making the saffron potatoes, cook the potatoes in boiling salted water for 8 minutes and drain well. Return the potatoes to the saucepan along with the saffron, stock, onion and 25 g/1 oz of the butter. Season to taste with salt and pepper and simmer uncovered for 10 minutes until the potatoes are tender.

Meanwhile, mix together the vinegar, olive oil, sugar and seasoning. Coat the tomatoes in the dressing. Arrange the tomatoes, either cut-side down on the barbecue or cut-side up in a foil-lined grill pan. Grill for 3–6 minutes (if cooking on the barbecue they will take 3–4 minutes if in the centre, or 5–6 minutes if towards the outside), basting occasionally, until tender.

Place the steaks on the barbecue and cook for 4–8 minutes, or to taste and depending on thickness. Or if using a frying pan, melt the butter then add the steaks and cook, again, according to personal preference.

Arrange the potatoes, if using, and tomatoes in the centre of 4 serving plates. Top with the steaks along with any pan juices. Sprinkle over the parsley and serve immediately.

Try This: FOR AN ALTERNATIVE: 74 FOR A FISH OR VEGETABLE OPTION: 46

Fillet Steaks with Tomato & Garlic Sauce

SERVES 4

700 g/1½ lb ripe tomatoes
2 garlic cloves
2 tbsp olive oil
2 tbsp freshly chopped basil
2 tbsp freshly

chopped oregano
2 tbsp red wine
salt and freshly ground
    black pepper
75 g/3 oz pitted black

olives, chopped
4 fillet steaks, about 175 g/6
    oz each in weight
salad or freshly cooked
    vegetables, to serve

Make a small cross on the top of each tomato and place in a large bowl. Cover with boiling water and leave for 2 minutes. Using a slotted spoon, remove the tomatoes and skin carefully. Repeat until all the tomatoes are skinned. Place on a chopping board, cut into quarters, remove the seeds and roughly chop, then reserve.

Peel and chop the garlic. Heat half the olive oil in a saucepan and cook the garlic for 30 seconds. Add the chopped tomatoes with the basil, oregano, red wine and season to taste with salt and pepper. Bring to the boil then reduce the heat, cover and simmer for 15 minutes, stirring occasionally, or until the sauce is reduced and thickened. Stir the olives into the sauce and keep warm while cooking the steaks.

Meanwhile, prepare the barbecue or, when ready to cook, lightly oil a griddle pan or heavy-based frying pan with the remaining olive oil. Cook the steaks for 2 minutes on each side to seal. Continue to cook the steaks for a further 2–4 minutes, depending on personal preference. Serve the steaks immediately with the garlic sauce and salad or freshly cooked vegetables.

Try This: FOR AN ALTERNATIVE: 72   FOR A FISH OR VEGETABLE OPTION: 118

Spicy Chicken Skewers with Mango Tabbouleh

SERVES 4

8 metal or wood skewers
400 g/14 oz chicken
    breast fillet
200 ml/7 fl oz natural
    yoghurt
1 garlic clove, peeled
    and crushed
1 small red chilli, deseeded
    and finely chopped

½ tsp ground turmeric
juice and finely grated rind
    of ½ lemon
sprigs of fresh mint,
    to garnish

For the mango tabbouleh:
175 g/6 oz bulgur wheat
1 tsp olive oil

juice of ½ lemon
½ red onion, finely chopped
1 ripe mango, halved, stoned,
    peeled and chopped
¼ cucumber, finely diced
2 tbsp freshly chopped parsley
2 tbsp freshly shredded mint
salt and finely ground
    black pepper

If using wooden skewers, soak them in cold water for at least 30 minutes. Cut the chicken into 5 x 1 cm/2 x ½ inch strips and place in a shallow dish.

Mix together the yoghurt, garlic, chilli, turmeric, lemon rind and juice. Pour over the chicken and toss to coat. Cover and leave to marinate in the refrigerator for up to 8 hours.

Meanwhile, preheat the barbecue, if using. To make the tabbouleh, put the bulgur wheat in a bowl. Pour over enough boiling water to cover. Put a plate over the bowl. Leave to soak for 20 minutes. Whisk together the oil and lemon juice in a bowl. Add the red onion and leave to marinate for 10 minutes. Drain the bulgur wheat and squeeze out any excess moisture in a clean tea towel. Add to the red onion with the mango, cucumber and herbs and season to taste with salt and pepper. Toss together.

Thread the chicken strips on to 8 wooden or metal skewers. Cook on a barbecue or under a hot grill for 8 minutes. Turn and brush with the marinade until the chicken is lightly browned and cooked through. Spoon the tabbouleh on to individual plates. Arrange the chicken skewers on top and garnish with the sprigs of mint. Serve warm or cold.

Try This: FOR AN ALTERNATIVE: 88 FOR A FISH OR VEGETABLE OPTION: 130

Cheesy Chicken Burgers

SERVES 6

1 tbsp sunflower oil
1 small onion, peeled
   and finely chopped
1 garlic clove, peeled
   and crushed
½ red pepper, deseeded and
   finely chopped
450 g/1 lb fresh chicken mince
2 tbsp 0%-fat Greek yoghurt
50 g/2 oz fresh
   brown breadcrumbs

1 tbsp freshly chopped herbs,
   such as parsley or tarragon
50 g/2 oz Cheshire
   cheese, crumbled
salt and freshly ground
   black pepper

**For the sweetcorn
   and carrot relish:**
200 g can sweetcorn, drained
1 carrot, peeled, grated

½ green chilli, deseeded
   and finely chopped
2 tsp cider vinegar
2 tsp light soft brown sugar

To serve:
wholemeal or granary rolls
lettuce
sliced tomatoes
mixed salad leaves

Prepare the barbecue or preheat the grill. Heat the oil in a frying pan and gently cook the onion and garlic for 5 minutes. Add the red pepper and cook for 5 minutes. Transfer into a mixing bowl. Add the chicken, yoghurt, breadcrumbs, herbs and cheese and season to taste with salt and pepper. Mix well. Divide the mixture equally into 6 and shape into burgers. Cover and chill in the refrigerator for at least 20 minutes.

To make the relish, put all the ingredients in a small saucepan with 1 tablespoon of water and heat gently, stirring occasionally, until all the sugar has dissolved. Cover and cook over a low heat for 2 minutes, then uncover and cook for a further minute, or until the relish is thick.

Place the burgers carefully directly onto the barbecue (or onto a lightly oiled griddle plate on the barbecue if you are worried about them breaking up), or place under a medium hot grill. Cook for 8–10 minutes on each side, or until browned and completely cooked through. (They will need longer if not directly on the barbecue.) Warm the rolls if liked, then split in half and fill with the burgers, lettuce, sliced tomatoes and the prepared relish. Serve immediately with the salad leaves.

Try This: FOR AN ALTERNATIVE: 80   FOR A FISH OR VEGETABLE OPTION: 124

Chilli Beef Burgers

SERVES 4

1 small red chilli pepper
450 g/1 lb lean minced beef
1 clove garlic, crushed
1 small onion, grated
2 tbsp freshly chopped
   coriander

1 tbsp vegetable oil,
   for brushing
125 g/4 oz rocket
20 Vietnamese mint leaves
20 g/¾ oz loosely packed
   fresh coriander leaves

1 tbsp chilli oil
salt and freshly ground
   black pepper
4 crusty rolls, halved
50 ml/2 fl oz Thai sweet chilli
   sauce (optional)

Prepare the barbecue, or line a grill rack with kitchen foil and preheat the grill 2–3 minutes before cooking. Cut the top off the chilli. Slit down the side and discard the seeds and membrane (the skin to which the seeds are attached). Finely chop the chilli.

In a bowl, combine the beef, garlic, chilli, onion and chopped coriander. Using wet hands, mix well. Divide into 4 portions and shape each portion into a patty, flattening it slightly to fit the size of the roll.

Brush both sides of the beef patties with vegetable oil and cook on the barbecue or under the grill for 3–4 minutes per side, until cooked through to the centre.

In a bowl, combine the rocket, mint and coriander. Drizzle with chilli oil and season with salt and pepper. Place the greens on the bottom halves of the rolls. Add the beef patties and drizzle with Thai sweet chilli sauce if desired. Add the tops of the rolls and serve.

Try This: FOR AN ALTERNATIVE: 78 FOR A FISH OR VEGETABLE OPTION: 50

Soy Beef Skewers

SERVES 3–4

12 bamboo skewers
250 g/9 oz sirloin or
　rump steak
5 tbsp soy sauce
2 tbsp oyster sauce

1 tsp sugar
2 tbsp mirin
2 tsp sesame oil
1 clove garlic, finely
　chopped

1 tbsp freshly chopped
　coriander
2 tbsp vegetable oil

Prepare the barbecue, or line a grill rack with kitchen foil and preheat the grill 2–3 minutes before cooking. Soak the skewers in cold water for 30 minutes, then drain.

Slice the steak into thin long strips, about 2.5 x 10 cm/1 x 4 inches. Thread strips onto skewers and place in a shallow nonmetallic dish.

In a bowl, combine 2 tablespoons of the soy sauce, the oyster sauce, sugar, mirin, sesame oil, garlic and coriander, and mix well.

Brush the marinade over the beef, cover with clingfilm and refrigerate for 30 minutes, then drain off the marinade.

Away from the hot coals, lightly brush the barbecue grill rack with oil. Cook the skewers on the barbecue or under the preheated grill for 2–3 minutes until tender, turning when necessary.

Remove from the grill and serve hot with the remaining soy sauce as a dipping sauce.

Turkey Escalopes with Apricot Chutney

SERVES 4

4 x 175–225 g/6–8 oz
   turkey steaks
1 tbsp plain flour
salt and freshly ground
   black pepper
1 tbsp olive oil
flat-leaf parsley sprigs,
   to garnish

orange wedges, to serve

For the apricot chutney:
125 g/4 oz no-need-to-soak
   dried apricots, chopped
1 red onion, peeled and
   finely chopped
1 tsp grated fresh root ginger

2 tbsp caster sugar
finely grated rind of ½
   orange
125 ml/4 fl oz fresh
   orange juice
125 ml/4 fl oz ruby port
1 whole clove

Prepare the barbecue. Put a turkey steak on to a sheet of non-pvc clingfilm or non-stick baking parchment. Cover with a second sheet. Using a rolling pin, gently pound the turkey until the meat is flattened to about 5 mm/ ¼ inch thick. Repeat to make 4 escalopes.

Mix the flour with the salt and pepper and use to lightly dust the turkey escalopes. Put the turkey escalopes on a board or baking tray and cover with a piece of non-pvc clingfilm or non-stick baking parchment. Chill in the refrigerator until ready to cook.

For the apricot chutney, put the apricots, onion, ginger, sugar, orange rind, orange juice, port and clove into a saucepan. Slowly bring to the boil and simmer, uncovered for 10 minutes, stirring occasionally, until thick and syrupy. Remove the clove and stir in the chopped coriander.

Cook the turkey escalopes, in 2 batches if necessary, on the barbecue or in an oiled and heated griddle pan, for 3–4 minutes on each side until golden brown and tender.

Spoon the chutney on to 4 individual serving plates. Place a turkey escalope on top of each spoonful of chutney. Garnish with sprigs of parsley and serve immediately with orange wedges.

Try This: FOR AN ALTERNATIVE: 76   FOR A FISH OR VEGETABLE OPTION: 36

Sticky–glazed Spatchcocked Poussins

SERVES 4

2 poussins, each about 700 g/1½ lb
salt and freshly ground black pepper
4 kumquats, thinly sliced (optional)
assorted salad leaves,

crusty bread or new potatoes, to serve

For the glaze:
zest of 1 small lemon, finely grated
1 tbsp lemon juice

1 tbsp dry sherry
2 tbsp clear honey
2 tbsp dark soy sauce
2 tbsp wholegrain mustard
1 tsp tomato purée
½ tsp Chinese five-spice powder

Prepare the barbecue or preheat the grill just before cooking, and soak 4 wooden skewers for 30 minutes. Place one of the poussins breast-side down on a board. Using poultry shears, cut down one side of the backbone. Cut down the other side of the backbone. Remove the bone. Open out the poussin and press down hard on the breast bone with the heel of your hand to break it and to flatten the poussin.

Thread 2 skewers crosswise through the bird to keep it flat, ensuring that each skewer goes through a wing and out through the leg on the opposite side. Repeat with the other bird. Season both sides of the bird with salt and pepper.

To make the glaze, mix together the lemon zest and juice, sherry, honey, soy sauce, mustard, tomato purée and Chinese five-spice powder and use to brush all over the poussins.

Place the poussins skin-side up on the barbecue or skin-side down on a grill rack and cook on a medium heat for 15 minutes, brushing halfway through with more glaze. Turn the poussins over and cook for 10 minutes. Brush again with glaze and cook for a further 15 minutes until well-browned and cooked through. If they start to brown too quickly, move the poussins to the edge of the barbecue or turn the grill down. Remove the skewers and cut each poussin in half along the breastbone. Serve immediately with the kumquat slices, if using, salad, crusty bread or new potatoes. If using a grill, you can grill the kumquats on top of the birds before serving.

Try This: FOR AN ALTERNATIVE: 90   FOR A FISH OR VEGETABLE OPTION: 60

Chicken & New Potatoes
on Rosemary Skewers

SERVES 4

8 thick fresh rosemary stems, at least 23 cm/ 9 inches long
3–4 tbsp extra-virgin olive oil
2 garlic cloves, peeled and crushed
1 tsp freshly chopped thyme

grated rind and juice of 1 lemon
salt and freshly ground black pepper
4 skinless chicken breast fillets
16 small new potatoes, peeled or scrubbed

8 very small onions or shallots, peeled
1 large yellow or red pepper, deseeded
lemon wedges, to garnish
parsley-flavoured cooked rice, to serve

Prepare the barbecue, or preheat the grill and line the grill rack with kitchen foil just before cooking. Strip the leaves from the rosemary stems, leaving about 5 cm/2 inches of soft leaves at the top. Chop the leaves coarsely and reserve. Using a sharp knife, cut the thicker woody ends of the stems to a point which can pierce the chicken pieces and potatoes. Blend the chopped rosemary, oil, garlic, thyme and lemon rind and juice in a shallow dish. Season to taste with salt and pepper. Cut the chicken into 4 cm/½ inch cubes, add to the flavoured oil and stir well. Cover, refrigerate for at least 30 minutes, turning occasionally.

Cook the potatoes in lightly salted boiling water for 10–12 minutes until just tender. Add the onions to the potatoes 2 minutes before the end of the cooking time. Drain, rinse under cold running water and leave to cool. Cut the pepper into 2.5 cm/1 inch squares.

Beginning with a piece of chicken and starting with the pointed end of the skewer, alternately thread equal amounts of chicken, potato, pepper and onion onto each rosemary skewer. Cover the leafy ends of the skewers with kitchen foil to stop them from burning. Do not thread the chicken and vegetables too closely together on the skewer or the chicken may not cook completely. Cook the kebabs for 15 minutes, or until tender and golden, turning and brushing lightly with a little extra marinade. Remove the kitchen foil, garnish with lemon wedges and serve on rice.

Try This: FOR AN ALTERNATIVE: 104   FOR A FISH OR VEGETABLE OPTION: 40

Spatchcocked Poussins with Garlic Sage Butter

SERVES 4

For the herb butter:
6 large garlic cloves
150 g/5 oz butter, softened
2 tbsp freshly snipped chives
2 tbsp freshly chopped sage
juice and grated rind of
   1 small lemon

salt and freshly ground
   black pepper

For the poussins:
4 spatchcocked poussins
2 tbsp extra-virgin olive oil

To garnish:
chives
fresh sage leaves

To serve:
grilled polenta
grilled tomatoes

Prepare the barbecue, or preheat the grill and line the grill rack with foil, just before cooking. Soak 8 wooden skewers 30 minutes before cooking. Put the garlic cloves in a small saucepan and cover with cold water. Bring to the boil, then simmer for 5 minutes, or until softened. Drain and cool slightly. Cut off the root end of each clove and squeeze the softened garlic into a bowl. Pound the garlic until smooth, then beat in the butter, chives, sage and lemon rind and juice. Season to taste with salt and pepper.

Using your fingertips, gently loosen the skin from each poussin breast by sliding your hand between the skin and the flesh. Push one quarter of the herb butter under the skin, spreading evenly over the breast and the top of the thighs. Pull the neck skin gently to tighten the skin over the breast and tuck under the bird. Repeat with the remaining birds and herb butter.

Thread 2 wooden skewers crossways through each bird, from one wing through the opposite leg, to keep the poussin flat. Repeat with the remaining birds, brush with the olive oil and season with salt and pepper. Arrange the poussins on the barbecue or grill rack and cook for 25 minutes, turning occasionally, until golden and crisp and the juices run clear when a thigh is pierced with a sharp knife or skewer. If they start to brown too quickly, move the poussins to the edge of the barbecue or turn the grill down. Garnish with chives and sage leaves and serve immediately with grilled polenta and a few grilled tomatoes.

Try This: FOR AN ALTERNATIVE: 86   FOR A FISH OR VEGETABLE OPTION: 32

Marinated Pheasant Breasts with Grilled Polenta

SERVES 4

3 tbsp extra-virgin olive oil
1 tbsp freshly chopped
    rosemary or sage leaves
½ tsp ground cinnamon
grated zest of 1 orange
salt and freshly ground

black pepper
8 pheasant or wood
    pigeon breasts
600 ml/1 pint water
125 g/4 oz quick-cook polenta
2 tbsp butter, diced

40 g/1½ oz Parmesan
    cheese, grated
1–2 tbsp freshly
    chopped parsley
assorted salad leaves and
    tomatoes, to serve

Prepare the barbecue, or preheat the grill just before cooking. Blend 2 tablespoons of the olive oil with the rosemary or sage, cinnamon and orange zest and season to taste with salt and pepper.

Place the pheasant breasts in a large, shallow dish, pour over the oil and marinate until required, turning occasionally.

Bring the water and 1 teaspoon of salt to the boil in a large, heavy-based saucepan. Slowly whisk in the polenta in a thin, steady stream. Reduce the heat and simmer for 5–10 minutes, or until very thick, stirring constantly. Stir the butter and cheese into the polenta, then the parsley and a little black pepper.

Turn the polenta out on to a lightly oiled, non-stick baking tray and spread into an even layer about 2 cm/¾ inch thick. Leave to cool, then chill in the refrigerator for about 1 hour, or until the polenta is chilled. Turn the cold polenta on to a work surface. Cut into 10 cm/4 inch squares. Brush with olive oil and arrange on the barbecue or grill rack. Cook for 2–3 minutes on each side until crisp and golden, then cut each square into triangles and keep warm.

Transfer the marinated pheasant breasts to the barbecue or grill rack and cook for at least 5 minutes, or until crisp and beginning to colour, turning once. Serve the pheasants immediately with the polenta triangles, salad leaves and tomatoes.

Try This: FOR AN ALTERNATIVE: 72 FOR A FISH OR VEGETABLE OPTION: 28

Mixed Satay Sticks

SERVES 4

8 bamboo skewers
12 large raw prawns
350 g/12 oz beef rump steak
1 tbsp lemon juice
1 garlic clove, peeled
   and crushed
salt
2 tsp soft dark brown sugar
1 tsp ground cumin

1 tsp ground coriander
¼ tsp ground turmeric
1 tbsp groundnut oil
fresh coriander leaves,
   to garnish

For the spicy peanut sauce:
1 shallot, peeled and very
   finely chopped

1 tsp demerara sugar
50 g/2 oz creamed
   coconut, chopped
pinch of chilli powder
1 tbsp dark soy sauce
125 g/4 oz crunchy
   peanut butter

Prepare the barbecue, or preheat the grill on high just before cooking. Soak the skewers in cold water for at least 30 minutes. Peel the prawns, leaving the tails on. Using a sharp knife, remove the black vein along the back of the prawns. Cut the beef into 1 cm/½ inch wide strips. Place the prawns and beef in separate bowls and sprinkle each with ½ tablespoon of the lemon juice. Mix together the garlic, pinch of salt, sugar, cumin, coriander, turmeric and groundnut oil to make a paste. Lightly brush over the prawns and beef. Cover and place in the refrigerator, to marinate for at least 30 minutes, but for longer if possible.

Meanwhile, make the sauce. Pour 125 ml/4 fl oz of water into a small saucepan, add the shallot and sugar and heat gently until the sugar has dissolved. Stir in the creamed coconut and chilli powder. When melted, remove from the heat and stir in the peanut butter. Leave to cool slightly, then spoon into a serving dish.

Thread 3 prawns each on to 4 skewers and divide the sliced beef between the remaining skewers. Cook the skewers on the barbecue or under the preheated grill for 4–5 minutes, turning occasionally. The prawns should be opaque and pink and the beef browned on the outside, but still pink in the centre. Transfer to warmed individual serving plates, garnish with a few fresh coriander leaves and serve immediately with the warm peanut sauce.

Try This: FOR AN ALTERNATIVE: 98   FOR A FISH OR VEGETABLE OPTION: 58

Chicken & Lamb Satay

SERVES 4

225 g/8 oz skinless, boneless chicken
225 g/8 oz lean lamb
16 bamboo skewers

For the marinade:
1 small onion, peeled and finely chopped
2 garlic cloves, peeled and crushed
2.5 cm/1 inch piece fresh root ginger, peeled and grated
4 tbsp soy sauce
1 tsp ground coriander
2 tsp dark brown sugar
2 tbsp lime juice
1 tbsp vegetable oil

For the peanut sauce:
300 ml/½ pint coconut milk
4 tbsp crunchy peanut butter
1 tbsp Thai fish sauce
1 tsp lime juice
1 tbsp chilli powder
1 tbsp brown sugar
salt and freshly ground black pepper

To garnish:
sprigs of fresh coriander
lime wedges

Cut the chicken and lamb into thin strips, about 7.5 cm/3 inches long and place in 2 shallow dishes. Blend all the marinade ingredients together, then pour half over the chicken and half over the lamb. Stir until lightly coated, then cover with clingfilm and leave to marinate in the refrigerator for at least 2 hours, turning occasionally.

Meanwhile, prepare the barbecue, or preheat the grill just before cooking. Soak the skewers in cold water for 30 minutes before required.

Remove the chicken and lamb from the marinade and thread on to the skewers. Reserve the marinade. Cook on the barbecue or under the preheated grill for 8–10 minutes or until thoroughly cooked, turning and brushing with the marinade.

Meanwhile, make the peanut sauce. Blend the coconut milk with the peanut butter, fish sauce, lime juice, chilli powder and sugar. Pour into a saucepan and cook gently for 5 minutes, stirring occasionally, then season to taste with salt and pepper. Garnish plates with coriander sprigs and lime wedges and serve the satays with the prepared sauce.

Try This: FOR AN ALTERNATIVE: 94   FOR A FISH OR VEGETABLE OPTION: 56

Malaysian Beef Satay

SERVES 4–6

450 g/1 lb beef steak,
such as rump or sirloin
1 tbsp vegetable oil
1 tsp fennel seeds
1 tsp fenugreek seeds
2 red chillies, deseeded and
chopped
2 garlic cloves, peeled and

crushed
1 tbsp Thai red curry paste
200 ml/7 fl oz coconut milk
8 wooden kebab skewers

For the satay sauce:
1 small red chilli, deseeded
and finely chopped

1 tbsp lime juice
50 ml/2 fl oz fish sauce
2 tbsp smooth peanut butter
1 tbsp roasted peanuts,
finely chopped
2 spring onions, trimmed
and finely chopped

Soak the wooden skewers in cold water for 30 minutes. Meanwhile, trim the steak, cut into narrow strips and place in a shallow dish.

Heat the oil in a small frying pan, add the seeds and fry for 30 seconds, or until they pop. Add the chillies, crushed garlic and curry paste and continue to fry, stirring, for 2 minutes. Remove from the heat and gradually blend in the coconut milk and allow to cool. Pour over the beef, cover lightly and leave to marinate in the refrigerator for at least 30 minutes.

Meanwhile prepare the barbecue, or, when ready to cook, preheat the grill to high and line the grill rack with kitchen foil. Drain the skewers and beef, reserving the remaining marinade. Thread the beef strips onto the skewers and place on the barbecue or under the preheated grill for 8–10 minutes, or until cooked to personal preference, brushing occasionally with the remaining marinade.

Meanwhile, place all the ingredients for the sauce in a small saucepan and heat gently for 3–5 minutes, stirring occasionally. Serve with the cooked beef.

Try This: FOR AN ALTERNATIVE: 96   FOR A FISH OR VEGETABLE OPTION: 38

Aromatic Duck Burgers on Potato Pancakes

SERVES 4

700 g/1½ lb boneless
   duck breasts
2 tbsp hoisin sauce
1 garlic clove, peeled and
   finely chopped
4 spring onions, trimmed
   and finely chopped
2 tbsp Japanese soy sauce

½ tsp Chinese five-spice
   powder
salt and freshly ground
   black pepper
freshly chopped coriander,
   to garnish
extra hoisin sauce, to serve

For the potato pancakes:
450 g/1 lb floury potatoes
1 small onion, peeled
   and grated
1 small egg, beaten
1 heaped tbsp plain flour

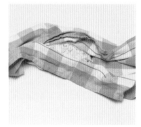

Peel off the thick layer of fat from the duck breasts and cut into small pieces. Put the fat in a small dry saucepan and set over a low heat for 10–15 minutes, or until the fat runs clear and the crackling goes crisp; reserve. Cut the duck meat into pieces and blend in a food processor until coarsely chopped. Spoon into a bowl and add the hoisin sauce, garlic, half the spring onions, soy sauce and Chinese five-spice powder. Season to taste with salt and pepper and shape into 4 burgers. Cover and chill in the refrigerator for 1 hour. Prepare the barbecue.

To make the potato pancakes, grate the potatoes into a large bowl, squeeze out the water with your hands, then put on a clean tea towel and twist the ends to squeeze out any remaining water. Return the potato to the bowl, add the onion and egg and mix well. Add the flour, salt and pepper. Stir to blend. Heat about 2 tablespoons of the clear duck fat on a flat griddle pan or frying pan on the barbecue (or on the hob), spoon the potato mixture into 2–4 pattie shapes and cook for 6 minutes, or until golden and crisp, turning once. Keep warm in the oven. Repeat with the remaining mixture, adding duck fat as needed.

Brush the burgers with a little of the duck fat and cook on the barbecue, or under a preheated grill, for 6–8 minutes or longer, turning once. Arrange 1–2 pancakes on a plate and top with a burger. Spoon over some hoisin sauce and garnish with the remaining spring onions and coriander.

Try This: FOR AN ALTERNATIVE: 80   FOR A FISH OR VEGETABLE OPTION: 48

Chicken Fillet
with Aubergine

SERVES 4

4 chicken breast fillets
4 spring onions, coarsely
    chopped
4 cloves garlic
1 tbsp freshly chopped basil
1 tbsp freshly chopped

coriander
85 ml/3 fl oz soy sauce
1 tsp five-spice powder
2 tbsp mirin
1 tbsp fish sauce
1 tsp sesame oil

1 tbsp rice wine
2 tsp sugar
6 aubergines
2 tbsp vegetable oil
50 g/2 oz mizuna leaves,
    rinsed

Place the chicken in a shallow nonmetallic dish. In a food processor, combine the spring onions, garlic, basil, coriander, soy sauce, five-spice powder, mirin, fish sauce, sesame oil, rice wine and sugar and process for about 30 seconds, until well blended. Pour the marinade over the chicken fillets, cover the dish with clingfilm and refrigerate for 2 hours.

Meanwhile, prepare the barbecue and slice the aubergines lengthwways into 2-mm/¹⁄₁₆-inch slices, cutting each slice in half also if the aubergines were quite large.

Drain the chicken, reserving the marinade. Away from the hot coals, lightly brush the barbecue grill with vegetable oil or heat the oil in a griddle pan. Cook the chicken fillets for 4–5 minutes on each side, until golden and tender, brushing with some of the reserved marinade during cooking. Test the chicken by piercing the thickest part with a skewer; the chicken is cooked if the juices run clear. Remove from the grill or pan.

Lightly brush the aubergine slices with oil and cook on the barbecue or in a griddle pan for 1–2 minutes each side, until golden and tender. Place the remaining marinade into a small saucepan, stir over a medium heat and bring to a boil; allow to boil for 1 minute, then set aside. To serve, arrange the mizuna leaves on serving plates, top with the aubergine slices and then the chicken fillets. Drizzle with warm marinade.

Try This: FOR AN ALTERNATIVE: 84 FOR A FISH OR VEGETABLE OPTION: 62

Skewered Chicken

SERVES 6

2 chickens, each about
   900 g/2 lb
125 ml/4 fl oz lemon juice
1 large onion, grated
2 tsp salt

freshly ground black pepper,
   or different flavoured
   peppers if liked
6 long sturdy wooden, or flat
   metal skewers

50 ml/2 fl oz butter, melted
1 tsp paprika
cherry tomatoes,
   to garnish

Using poultry shears or a very sharp knife, cut each chicken in half lengthwise and remove the backbone. Cut each half into six pieces that are nearly equal in size: halve breast pieces and thighs, chop off the bony end of the leg, and leave the wing intact. Put the chicken pieces in a nonmetallic dish or bowl.

In a bowl, combine the lemon juice, grated onion, salt and pepper(s) to taste. Pour over the chicken pieces, turning them in the marinade to coat. Cover the dish with clingfilm and marinate for 3–4 hours in the refrigerator, turning the chicken occasionally.

Prepare the barbecue, preferably with charcoal, and, if using wooden skewers, soak them in cold water for 30 minutes.

Thread the chicken onto the skewers, placing the thicker pieces in the centre, and packing all the pieces close together. In a small bowl, combine the melted butter with the paprika and brush over the chicken. Cook the chicken on the barbecue, basting frequently with the butter mixture and turning often, for 15–20 minutes or until the chicken is cooked through. Remove the chicken from the skewers if desired and garnish with blistered cherry tomatoes.

To blister cherry tomatoes, cut an 'X' on the bottom of each tomato and thread onto skewers if necessary. Brush with melted butter and cook on the barbecue until the skin blisters and browns lightly.

Try This: FOR AN ALTERNATIVE: 76   FOR A FISH OR VEGETABLE OPTION: 30

Barbecue Pork Fillet

SERVES 4

2 tbsp clear honey
2 tbsp hoisin sauce
2 tsp tomato purée
2.5 cm/1 inch piece fresh
    root ginger, peeled
    and chopped
450 g/1 lb pork tenderloin
salad, to serve (optional)

For the stir-fried veg:
3 tbsp vegetable oil
1 garlic clove, peeled
    and chopped
1 bunch spring onions,
    trimmed and chopped
1 red pepper, deseeded and
    cut into chunks
1 yellow pepper, deseeded

and cut into chunks
350 g/12 oz cooked
    long-grain rice
125 g/4 oz frozen peas, thawed
2 tbsp light soy sauce
1 tbsp sesame oil
50 g/2 oz toasted
    flaked almonds

Prepare a covered barbecue, or preheat the oven to 200°C/400°F/Gas Mark 6, 15 minutes before cooking. Mix together the honey, hoisin sauce, tomato purée and ginger in a bowl. Trim the pork, discarding any sinew or fat. Place in a shallow dish and spread the marinade over the pork to cover completely. Cover with clingfilm and chill in the refrigerator for 4 hours, turning occasionally.

Remove the pork from the marinade and place it on a large piece of kitchen foil, turning up the sides to envelope it in a parcel, or place it in a roasting tin. Reserve the marinade. Cook on the barbecue with the lid on, or in the preheated oven, for 20–25 minutes, or until the pork is tender and the juices run clear when pierced with a skewer. Baste occasionally during cooking with the reserved marinade. Remove the pork from the barbecue or oven, leave to rest for 5 minutes, then slice thinly and keep warm.

Meanwhile, heat a wok or large frying pan, add the vegetable oil and when hot, add the garlic, spring onions and peppers and stir-fry for 4 minutes or until softened. Add the rice and peas and stir-fry for 2 minutes. Add the soy sauce, sesame oil and flaked almonds and stir-fry for 30 seconds or until heated through. Tip into a warmed serving dish and top with the sliced pork. Serve immediately.

Try This: FOR AN ALTERNATIVE: 108   FOR A FISH OR VEGETABLE OPTION: 34

Sweet–&–Sour Spareribs

SERVES 4

1.6 kg/3½ lb pork spareribs
4 tbsp clear honey
1 tbsp Worcestershire sauce
1 tsp Chinese five-
   spice powder

4 tbsp soy sauce
2½ tbsp dry sherry
1 tsp chilli sauce
2 garlic cloves, peeled
   and chopped

1½ tbsp tomato purée
1 tsp dry mustard powder
   (optional)
spring onion curls,
   to garnish

Prepare a covered barbecue, or preheat the oven to 200°C/400°F/Gas Mark 6, 15 minutes before cooking. If necessary, place the ribs on a chopping board and using a sharp knife, cut the joint in between the ribs, to form single ribs. Place the ribs in a shallow dish in a single layer.

Spoon the honey, the Worcestershire sauce, Chinese five-spice powder with the soy sauce, sherry and chilli sauce into a small saucepan and heat gently, stirring until smooth. Stir in the chopped garlic, the tomato purée and mustard powder, if using.

Pour the honey mixture over the ribs and spoon over until the ribs are coated evenly. Cover with clingfilm and leave to marinate overnight in the refrigerator, occasionally spooning the marinade over the ribs.

When ready to cook, remove the ribs from the marinade and place (wrapped in foil to avoid burning if you prefer) on the coolest part of the barbecue with the lid closed, or in a shallow roasting tin in the oven with a little more marinade spooned over. Reserve the remainder of the marinade. Cook for 35–40 minutes, or until cooked and the outsides are crisp. Baste occasionally with the reserved marinade during cooking. Garnish with a few spring onion curls and serve immediately, either as a starter or as a meat accompaniment.

Try This: FOR AN ALTERNATIVE: 106   FOR A FISH OR VEGETABLE OPTION: 124

Thai Chicken Wings

SERVES 4

4 tbsp clear honey
1 tbsp chilli sauce
1 garlic clove, peeled
    and crushed
1 tsp freshly grated
    root ginger
1 lemon grass stalk, outer
    leaves discarded and

finely chopped
2 tbsp lime zest
3–4 tbsp freshly squeezed
    lime juice
1 tbsp light soy sauce
1 tsp ground cumin
1 tsp ground coriander
¼ tsp ground cinnamon

1.4 kg/3 lb chicken wings
    (about 12 large wings)
6 tbsp mayonnaise
2 tbsp freshly chopped
    coriander
lemon or lime wedges,
    to garnish

Prepare a covered barbecue, or preheat the oven to 190°C/375°F/Gas Mark 5, 10 minutes before cooking. In a small saucepan, mix together the honey, chilli sauce, garlic, ginger, lemon grass, 1 tablespoon of the lime zest and 2 tablespoons of the lime juice with the soy sauce, cumin, coriander and cinnamon. Heat gently until just starting to bubble, then remove from the heat and leave to cool.

Prepare the chicken wings by folding the tips back under the thickest part of the meat to form a triangle. Arrange in a shallow ovenproof dish. Pour over the honey mixture, turning the wings to ensure that they are all well coated. Cover with clingfilm and leave to marinate in the refrigerator for 4 hours or overnight, turning once or twice.

Mix together the mayonnaise with the remaining lime zest and juice and the coriander. Leave to let the flavours develop while the wings are cooking.

Arrange the wings on the barbecue in foil parcels, or on a rack set over a kitchen-foil-lined roasting tin. Cook in a covered barbecue, or roast at the top of the preheated oven, for 50–60 minutes, or until the wings are tender and golden, basting once or twice with the remaining marinade and turning once. Remove from the barbecue or oven. Garnish the wings with lemon or lime wedges and serve immediately with the mayonnaise.

Try This: FOR AN ALTERNATIVE: 86 FOR A FISH OR VEGETABLE OPTION: 52

Vegetables

Marinated Vegetable Kebabs

SERVES 4

8 wooden skewers
2 small courgettes, cut into
2 cm/¾ inch pieces
½ green pepper, deseeded
and cut into 2.5 cm/1
inch pieces
½ red pepper, deseeded
and cut into 2.5 cm/
1 inch pieces
½ yellow pepper, deseeded
and cut into 2.5 cm/

1 inch pieces
8 baby onions, peeled
8 button mushrooms
8 cherry tomatoes
freshly chopped parsley,
to garnish
freshly cooked couscous,
to serve

For the marinade:
1 tbsp light olive oil

4 tbsp dry sherry
2 tbsp light soy sauce
1 red chilli, deseeded and
finely chopped
2 garlic cloves, peeled
and crushed
2.5 cm/1 inch piece root
ginger, peeled and
finely grated

Soak the skewers in cold water for 30 minutes, then drain. Place the courgettes, peppers and baby onions in a pan of just boiled water. Bring back to the boil and simmer for about 30 seconds. Drain and rinse the cooked vegetables in cold water and dry on absorbent kitchen paper. Thread the cooked vegetables and the mushrooms and tomatoes alternately on to the skewers and place in a large shallow dish.

Make the marinade by whisking all the ingredients together until thoroughly blended. Pour the marinade evenly over the kebabs, then chill in the refrigerator for at least 1 hour. Spoon the marinade over the kebabs occasionally during this time. Meanwhile, prepare the barbecue.

Place the kebabs on a hot barbecue or in a hot griddle pan and cook gently for 10–12 minutes. Turn the kebabs frequently and brush with the marinade when needed. When the vegetables are tender, sprinkle over the chopped parsley and serve immediately with couscous.

Try This: FOR AN ALTERNATIVE: 130   FOR A FISH OR MEAT OPTION: 38

Spanish Tomatoes

SERVES 4

175 g/6 oz whole-grain rice
600 ml/1 pint
   vegetable stock
2 tsp sunflower oil
2 shallots, peeled and
   finely chopped
1 garlic clove, peeled
   and crushed

1 green pepper, deseeded
   and cut into small dice
1 red chilli, deseeded and
   finely chopped
50 g/2 oz button mushrooms
   finely chopped
1 tbsp freshly
   chopped oregano

salt and freshly ground
   black pepper
4 large ripe beef tomatoes
1 large egg, beaten
1 tsp caster sugar
basil leaves, to garnish
crusty bread, to serve

Prepare the barbecue (covered if available), or preheat the oven to 180°C/350°F/Gas Mark 4. Place the rice in a saucepan, pour over the vegetable stock and bring to the boil. Simmer for 30 minutes or until the rice is tender. Drain and turn into a mixing bowl.

Add 1 teaspoon of sunflower oil to a small, non-stick pan and gently fry the shallots, garlic, pepper, chilli and mushrooms for 2 minutes. Add to the rice with the chopped oregano. Season with plenty of salt and pepper.

Slice the top off each tomato. Cut and scoop out the flesh, removing the hard core. Pass the tomato flesh through a sieve. Add 1 tablespoon of the juice to the rice mixture. Stir in the beaten egg and mix. Sprinkle a little sugar in the base of each tomato. Pile the rice mixture into the shells.

If using an uncovered barbecue, place the tomatoes in 4 squares of kitchen foil big enough to be folded up into roomy parcels, or if using a covered barbecue or an oven place in a baking dish. Pour a little cold water around the tomatoes, replace their lids and drizzle a few drops of oil over the tops. Close the foil parcels, if using. Cook for about 25 minutes. Garnish with the basil leaves and season with black pepper and serve immediately with crusty bread.

Try This: FOR AN ALTERNATIVE: 118   FOR A FISH OR MEAT OPTION: 72

Italian Tomatoes with Curly Endive & Radicchio

SERVES 4

1 tsp olive oil
4 beef tomatoes
salt
50 g/2 oz fresh white
breadcrumbs
1 tbsp freshly
snipped chives
1 tbsp freshly

chopped parsley
125 g/4 oz button
mushrooms,
finely chopped
salt and freshly ground
black pepper
25 g/1 oz Parmesan
cheese, grated

For the salad:
½ curly endive lettuce
½ small piece of radicchio
2 tbsp olive oil
1 tsp balsamic vinegar
salt and freshly ground
black pepper

Prepare the barbecue (covered if available), or preheat oven to 190°C/375°F/Gas Mark 5. Lightly oil 4 squares of kitchen foil big enough to be folded up around each tomato into roomy parcels, or a baking tray (for use in the covered barcecue or oven), with the teaspoon of oil. Slice the tops off the tomatoes and remove all the tomato flesh and sieve into a large bowl. Sprinkle a little salt inside the tomato shells and then place them upside down on a plate while the filling is prepared.

Mix the sieved tomato with the breadcrumbs, fresh herbs and mushrooms and season well with salt and pepper. Place the tomato shells on the prepared kitchen foil or baking tray and fill with the tomato and mushroom mixture. Sprinkle the cheese on the top, close the foil parcels, if using, and cook on/in the barbecue or in the preheated oven for 15–20 minutes, until golden brown.

Meanwhile, prepare the salad. Arrange the endive and radicchio on individual serving plates and mix the remaining ingredients together in a small bowl to make the dressing. Season to taste.

When the tomatoes are cooked, allow to rest for 5 minutes, then place on the prepared plates and drizzle over a little dressing. Serve warm.

Stuffed Onions with Pine Nuts

SERVES 4

4 medium onions, peeled
2 garlic cloves,
    peeled and crushed
2 tbsp fresh
    brown breadcrumbs
2 tbsp white breadcrumbs

25 g/1 oz sultanas
25 g/1 oz pine nuts
50 g/2 oz hard cheese
    such as Edam or
    Cheddar, grated
2 tbsp freshly

chopped parsley
1 medium egg, beaten
salt and freshly ground
    black pepper
salad leaves, to serve

Prepare the barbecue, or preheat the oven to 200°C/400°F/Gas Mark 6.
Bring a pan of water to the boil, add the onions and cook gently for about 15 minutes.

Drain well. Allow the onions to cool, then slice each one in half horizontally.
Scoop out most of the onion flesh but leave a reasonably firm shell.

Chop up 4 tablespoons of the onion flesh and place in a bowl with the crushed garlic,
breadcrumbs, sultanas, pine nuts, grated cheese and parsley.

Mix the breadcrumb mixture together thoroughly. Bind together with as much of the beaten
egg as necessary to make a firm filling. Season to taste with salt and pepper.

Pile the mixture back into the onion shells and top with the grated cheese. Place on 4 squares
of kitchen foil big enough to fold easily around each, and create 4 parcels for the barbecue, or
place on an oiled baking tray for the oven. Cook on the barbecue or in the preheated oven for
20–30 minutes or until golden brown. Serve immediately with the salad leaves. If cooking on
a barbecue you may wish to finish them off under the grill to achieve a more crisp top.

   Try This: FOR AN ALTERNATIVE: 122   FOR A FISH OR MEAT OPTION: 44

Rice–filled Peppers

SERVES 4

325 g/11 oz ripe tomatoes
2 tbsp olive oil
1 onion, peeled and
    chopped
1 garlic clove, peeled
    and crushed
½ tsp dark muscovado sugar

125 g/4 oz cooked
    long-grain rice
50 g/2 oz pine nuts, toasted
1 tbsp freshly chopped
    oregano
salt and freshly ground
    black pepper

2 large red peppers
2 large yellow peppers

To serve:
mixed salad
crusty bread

Prepare the barbecue (covered if available), or preheat the oven to 200°C/400°F/Gas Mark 6. Put the tomatoes in a small bowl and pour over boiling water to cover. Leave for 1 minute, then drain. Plunge the tomatoes into cold water to cool, then peel off the skins. Quarter, remove the seeds and chop.

Heat the olive oil in a frying pan, and cook the onion gently for 10 minutes, until softened. Add the garlic, chopped tomatoes and sugar. Gently cook the tomato mixture for 10 minutes until thickened. Remove from the heat and stir the rice, pine nuts and oregano into the sauce. Season to taste with salt and pepper.

Halve the peppers lengthways, cutting through and leaving the stem on. Remove the seeds and cores, then put the peppers on the barbecue rack or in a lightly oiled roasting tin, cut-side down and cook in the barbecue or the preheated oven for about 10 minutes.

Spoon in the filling to the peppers, then, if using an uncovered barbecue, wrap the tomatoes in foil parcels, or if using a covered barbecue or an oven return to the roasting tin and cover with kitchen foil. Cook for 15 minutes, or until the peppers are very tender, opening the parcels or removing the foil for the last 5 miuntes. Serve one red pepper half and one yellow pepper half per person with a mixed salad and plenty of warmed, crusty bread.

Try This: FOR AN ALTERNATIVE: 120   FOR A FISH OR MEAT OPTION: 50

Sweet Potato Cakes with Mango & Tomato Salsa

SERVES 4

700 g/1½ lb sweet potatoes, peeled and cut into large chunks
salt and freshly ground black pepper
25 g/1 oz butter
1 onion, peeled and chopped
1 garlic clove, peeled and crushed

pinch of freshly grated nutmeg
1 medium egg, beaten
50 g/2 oz quick-cook polenta
2 tbsp sunflower oil

For the salsa:
1 ripe mango, peeled, stoned and diced
6 cherry tomatoes,

cut in wedges
4 spring onions, trimmed and thinly sliced
1 red chilli, deseeded and finely chopped
finely grated rind and juice of ½ lime
2 tbsp freshly chopped mint
1 tsp clear honey
salad leaves, to serve

Prepare the barbecue. Steam or cook the sweet potatoes in lightly salted boiling water for 15–20 minutes, until tender. Drain well, then mash until smooth.

Melt the butter in a saucepan. Add the onion and garlic and cook gently for 10 minutes until soft. Add to the mashed sweet potato and season with the nutmeg, salt and pepper. Stir together until mixed thoroughly. Leave to cool.

Shape the mixture into four oval potato cakes, about 2.5 cm/1 inch thick. Dip first in the beaten egg, allowing the excess to fall back into the bowl, then coat in the polenta. Refrigerate for at least 30 minutes.

Meanwhile, mix together all the ingredients for the salsa. Spoon into a serving bowl, cover with clingfilm and leave at room temperature to allow the flavours to develop.

Heat the oil in a flat barbecue tray or a frying pan on the barbecue or on the hob and cook the potato cakes for 4–5 minutes on each side. Serve with the salsa and salad leaves.

Try This: FOR AN ALTERNATIVE: 126   FOR A FISH OR MEAT OPTION: 48

Aduki Bean & Rice Burgers

SERVES 4

2½ tbsp sunflower oil
1 medium onion, peeled and
    very finely chopped
1 garlic clove, peeled
    and crushed
1 tsp curry paste
225 g/8 oz basmati rice
400 g can aduki beans,
    drained and rinsed
225 ml/8 fl oz vegetable
    stock

125 g/4 oz firm tofu,
    crumbled
1 tsp garam masala
2 tbsp freshly chopped
    coriander
salt and freshly ground
    black pepper

For the carrot raita:
2 large carrots, peeled
    and grated

½ cucumber, cut into
    tiny dice
150 ml/¼ pint Greek yogurt

To serve:
wholemeal baps
tomato slices
lettuce leaves

Heat 1 tablespoon of the oil in a saucepan and gently cook the onion for 10 minutes until soft. Add the garlic and curry paste and cook for a few more seconds. Stir in the rice and beans. Pour in the stock, bring to the boil and simmer for 12 minutes, or until all the stock has been absorbed – do not lift the lid for the first 10 minutes of cooking. Reserve.

Lightly mash the tofu. Add to the rice mixture with the garam masala, coriander, salt and pepper. Mix. Divide the mixture into eight and shape into burgers. Chill in the refrigerator for 30 minutes.

Meanwhile, make the raita. Mix together the carrots, cucumber and Greek yogurt. Spoon into a small bowl and chill in the refrigerator until ready to serve.

Heat the remaining oil in a flat barbecue tray or a frying pan on the barbecue or on the hob. Fry the burgers, in batches if necessary, for 4–5 minutes on each side, or until lightly browned. Serve in the baps with tomato slices and lettuce. Accompany with the raita.

Try This: FOR AN ALTERNATIVE: 124   FOR A FISH OR MEAT OPTION: 80

Hot Chicory & Pears

SERVES 4

50 g/2 oz unblanched
   almonds, roughly
   chopped
4 small heads of chicory
2 tbsp olive oil
1 tbsp walnut oil

2 firm ripe dessert pears
2 tsp lemon juice
1 tsp freshly chopped
   oregano.
salt and freshly ground
   black pepper

freshly chopped oregano,
   to garnish
warmed ciabatta bread,
   to serve

Prepare the barbecue or preheat the grill to hot. Fry the chopped almonds in a little oil in a pan on the barbecue or cook under a grill on a foil-lined grill pan. Cook for about 3 minutes, moving the almonds around occasionally, until lightly browned. Reserve.

Halve the chicory lengthways and cut out the cores. Mix together the olive and walnut oils. Brush about 2 tablespoons all over the chicory.

Put the chicory on the barbecue in foil parcels, or on a grill pan, and cook on a hot heat for 2–3 minutes, or until beginning to char. Turn and cook for a further 1–2 minutes, then turn again.

Peel, core and thickly slice the pears. Brush with 1 tablespoon of the oils, then place the pears on top of the chicory. Cook for a further 3–4 minutes, or until both the chicory and pears are soft.

Transfer the chicory and pears to 4 warmed serving plates. Whisk together the remaining oil, lemon juice and oregano and season to taste with salt and pepper.

Drizzle the dressing over the chicory and pears and scatter with the toasted almonds. Garnish with fresh oregano and serve with ciabatta bread.

Try This: FOR AN ALTERNATIVE: 122   FOR A FISH OR MEAT OPTION: 52

Tortellini, Cherry Tomato & Mozzarella Skewers

SERVES 6

8 wooden skewers
250 g/9 oz mixed green and
plain cheese or vegetable-
filled fresh tortellini
150 ml/¼ pint extra
virgin olive oil

2 garlic cloves, peeled
and crushed
pinch dried thyme or basil
salt and freshly ground
black pepper
225 g/8 oz cherry tomatoes

450 g/1 lb mozzarella, cut
into 2.5 cm/1 inch cubes
basil leaves, to garnish
dressed salad leaves,
to serve

Soak the skewers in cold water for at least 30 minutes. Prepare the barbecue, or preheat the grill and line the grill pan with kitchen foil, just before cooking. Bring a large pan of lightly salted water to a rolling boil. Add the tortellini and cook according to the packet instructions, or until 'al dente'. Drain, rinse under cold running water, drain again and toss with 2 tablespoons of the olive oil and reserve.

Pour the remaining olive oil into a small bowl. Add the crushed garlic and thyme or basil, then blend well. Season to taste with salt and black pepper and reserve.

To assemble the skewers, thread the tortellini alternately with the cherry tomatoes and cubes of mozzarella. Brush the skewers on all sides with the olive oil mixture then either place on the hot barbecue or place in the grill rack under the preheated grill.

Cook the skewers for about 5 minutes, or until they begin to turn golden, turning them halfway through cooking. Arrange two skewers on each plate and garnish with a few basil leaves. Serve immediately with dressed salad leaves.

Try This: FOR AN ALTERNATIVE: 114 FOR A FISH OR MEAT OPTION: 88

Side Dishes & Salads

Roasted Aubergine Dip with Pitta Strips

SERVES 4

4 pitta breads
2 large aubergines
1 garlic clove, peeled
¼ tsp sesame oil

1 tbsp lemon juice
½ tsp ground cumin
salt and freshly ground
    black pepper

2 tbsp freshly
    chopped parsley
fresh salad leaves,
    to serve

Preheat the oven to 180°C/350°F/Gas Mark 4. On a chopping board cut the pitta breads into strips. Spread the bread in a single layer on to a large baking tray. Cook in the preheated oven for 15 minutes until golden and crisp. Leave to cool on a wire cooling rack.

Trim the aubergines, rinse lightly and reserve. Heat the oil in a griddle pan until almost smoking. Cook the aubergines and garlic for about 15 minutes. Turn the aubergines frequently, until very tender with wrinkled and charred skins. Remove from heat. Leave to cool. (You could grill the aubergines on the barbecue if wished.)

When the aubergines are cool enough to handle, cut in half and scoop out the cooked flesh and place in a food processor. Squeeze the softened garlic flesh from the papery skin and add to the aubergine.

Blend the aubergine and garlic until smooth, then add the sesame oil, lemon juice and cumin and blend again to mix. Season to taste with salt and pepper, stir in the parsley and serve with the pitta strips and mixed salad leaves.

Try This: FOR AN ALTERNATIVE: 136 FOR THE BARBECUE GRILL: 44

Aubergine & Yogurt Dip

MAKES 600 ml/1 pint

2 x 225 g/8 oz aubergines
1 tbsp light olive oil
1 tbsp lemon juice
2 garlic cloves, peeled
    and crushed
190 g jar pimentos, drained

150 ml/¼ pint
    natural yogurt
salt and freshly ground
    black pepper
25 g/1 oz black olives, pitted
    and chopped

225 g/8 oz cauliflower florets
225 g/8 oz broccoli florets
125 g/4 oz carrots,
    peeled and cut into
    5 cm/2 inch strips

Preheat the oven to 200°C/400°F/Gas Mark 6. Pierce the skin of the aubergines with a fork and place on a baking tray. Cook for 40 minutes or until very soft.

Cool the aubergines, then cut in half, and scoop out the flesh and tip into a bowl. Mash the aubergine with the olive oil, lemon juice and garlic until smooth or blend for a few seconds in a food processor.

Chop the pimentos into small cubes and add to the aubergine mixture. When blended add the yogurt. Stir well and season to taste with salt and pepper. Add the chopped olives and leave in the refrigerator to chill for at least 30 minutes.

Place the cauliflower and broccoli florets and carrot strips into a pan and cover with boiling water. Simmer for 2 minutes, then rinse in cold water. Drain and serve as crudités to accompany the dip.

Try This: FOR AN ALTERNATIVE: 134   FOR THE BARBECUE GRILL: 58

Sweet Potato Crisps with Mango Salsa

SERVES 6

For the salsa:
1 large ripe mango, peeled, stoned and cut into small cubes
8 cherry tomatoes, quartered
½ cucumber, peeled if preferred and finely diced
1 red onion, peeled and finely chopped
pinch of sugar
1 red chilli, deseeded and finely chopped
2 tbsp rice vinegar

2 tbsp olive oil
grated rind and juice of 1 lime
450 g/1 lb sweet potatoes, peeled and thinly sliced
vegetable oil, for deep frying
sea salt
2 tbsp freshly chopped mint

To make the salsa, mix the mango with the tomatoes, cucumber and onion. Add the sugar, chilli, vinegar, oil and the lime rind and juice. Mix together thoroughly, cover and leave for 45–50 minutes.

Soak the potatoes in cold water for 40 minutes to remove as much of the excess starch as possible. Drain and dry thoroughly in a clean tea towel, or absorbent kitchen paper.

Heat the oil to 190°C/375°F in a deep fryer. When at the correct temperature, place half the potatoes in the frying basket, then carefully lower the potatoes into the hot oil and cook for 4–5 minutes, or until they are golden brown, shaking the basket every minute so that they do not stick together.

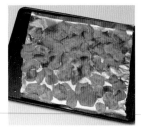

Drain the potato crisps on absorbent kitchen paper, sprinkle with sea salt and place under a preheated moderate grill for a few seconds to dry out. Repeat with the remaining potatoes. Stir the mint into the salsa and serve with the potato crisps.

Try This: FOR AN ALTERNATIVE: 148   FOR THE BARBECUE GRILL: 66

Stuffed Vine Leaves

SERVES 6–8

150 g/5 oz long-grain rice
225 g/8 oz fresh or preserved vine leaves
225 g/8 oz red onion, peeled and finely chopped
3 baby leeks, trimmed and finely sliced
25 g/1 oz freshly chopped parsley

25 g/1 oz freshly chopped mint
25 g/1 oz freshly chopped dill
150 ml/¼ pint extra-virgin olive oil
salt and freshly ground black pepper
50 g/2 oz currants
50 g/2 oz ready-to-eat dried

apricots, finely chopped
25 g/1 oz pine nuts
juice of 1 lemon
600–750 ml/1–1¼ pints boiling stock
lemon wedges or slices, to garnish
4 tbsp Greek-style yogurt, to serve

Soak the rice in cold water for 30 minutes. If using fresh vine leaves, blanch 5–6 leaves at a time in salted boiling water for a minute. Rinse and drain. If using preserved vine leaves, soak in tepid water for at least 20 minutes, drain, rinse and pat dry with absorbent kitchen paper.

Mix the onion and leeks with the herbs and half the oil. Add the drained rice, mix and season to taste with salt and pepper. Stir in the currants, apricots, pine nuts and lemon juice. Spoon 1 teaspoon of the filling on to the stalk end of each leaf. Roll, tucking the side flaps into the centre to create a neat parcel; do not roll too tight. Continue until all the filling is used.

Layer half the remaining vine leaves over the base of a large frying pan. Pack the little parcels in the frying pan and cover with the remaining leaves.

Pour in enough stock to just cover the vine leaves, add a pinch of salt and bring to the boil. Reduce the heat, cover and simmer for 45–55 minutes, or until the rice is sticky and tender. Leave to stand for 10 minutes. Drain the stock. Garnish with lemon wedges and serve hot with the Greek yogurt.

Try This: FOR AN ALTERNATIVE: 162   FOR THE BARBECUE GRILL: 102

Creamy Puy Lentils

SERVES 4

225 g/8 oz puy lentils
1 tbsp olive oil
1 garlic clove, peeled and
    finely chopped
zest and juice of 1 lemon
1 tsp wholegrain mustard
1 tbsp freshly

chopped tarragon
3 tbsp crème fraîche
salt and freshly ground
    black pepper
2 small tomatoes, deseeded
    and chopped
50 g/2 oz pitted black olives

1 tbsp freshly
    chopped parsley

To garnish:
sprigs of fresh tarragon
lemon wedges

Put the lentils in a saucepan with plenty of cold water and bring to the boil. Boil rapidly for 10 minutes, reduce the heat and simmer gently for a further 20 minutes until just tender. Drain well.

Meanwhile, prepare the dressing. Heat the oil in a frying pan over a medium heat. Add the garlic and cook for about a minute until just beginning to brown. Add the lemon zest and juice.

Add the mustard and cook for a further 30 seconds. Add the tarragon and crème fraîche and season to taste with salt and pepper.

Simmer and add the drained lentils, tomatoes and olives. Transfer to a serving dish and sprinkle the chopped parsley on top.

Garnish the lentils with the tarragon sprigs and the lemon wedges and serve immediately.

Try This: FOR AN ALTERNATIVE: 182   FOR THE BARBECUE GRILL: 28

Peperonata

SERVES 6

2 red peppers
2 yellow peppers
450 g/1 lb waxy potatoes
1 large onion
2 tbsp good quality virgin
  olive oil

700 g/1½ lb tomatoes,
  peeled, deseeded
  and chopped
2 small courgettes
50 g/2 oz pitted black
  olives, quartered

small handful basil leaves
salt and freshly ground
  black pepper
crusty bread, to serve

Prepare the peppers by halving them lengthwise and removing the stems, seeds, and membranes.

Cut the peppers lengthwise into strips about 1 cm/½ inch wide. Peel the potatoes and cut into rough dice, about 2.5–3 cm/1–1¼ inch across. Cut the onion lengthwise into eight wedges.

Heat the olive oil in a large saucepan over a medium heat. Add the onion and cook for about 5 minutes, or until starting to brown.

Add the peppers, potatoes, tomatoes, courgettes, black olives and about four torn basil leaves. Season to taste with salt and pepper.

Stir the mixture, cover and cook over a very low heat for about 40 minutes, or until the vegetables are tender but still hold their shape. Garnish with the remaining basil. Transfer to a serving bowl and serve immediately, with chunks of crusty bread.

Try This: FOR AN ALTERNATIVE: 202   FOR THE BARBECUE GRILL: 74

Coleslaw

SERVES 6

175 g/6 oz white cabbage
1 medium red onion, peeled
175 g/6 oz carrot, peeled
175 g/6 oz celeriac, peeled
2 celery stalks, trimmed

75 g/3 oz golden sultanas

**For the yogurt &
   herb dressing:**
150 ml/¼ pint natural yogurt

1 garlic clove, peeled
   and crushed
1 tbsp lemon juice
1 tsp clear honey
1 tbsp freshly snipped chives

Remove the hard core from the cabbage with a small knife and shred finely. Slice the onion finely and coarsely grate the carrot. Place the raw vegetables in a large bowl and mix together.

Cut the celeriac into thin strips and simmer in boiling water for about 2 minutes. Drain the celeriac and rinse thoroughly with cold water.

Chop the celery and add to the bowl with the celeriac and sultanas and mix well.

Make the yogurt and herb dressing by briskly whisking the yogurt, garlic, lemon juice, honey and chives together.

Pour the dressing over the top of the salad. Stir the vegetables thoroughly to coat evenly and serve.

Try This: FOR AN ALTERNATIVE: 176 FOR THE BARBECUE GRILL: 78

Crispy Baked Potatoes
with Serrano Ham

SERVES 4

4 large baking potatoes
4 tsp crème fraîche
salt and freshly ground
    black pepper
50 g/2 oz lean serrano ham
    or prosciutto, with fat

removed
50 g/2 oz cooked baby
    broad beans
50 g/2 oz cooked
    carrots, diced
50 g/2 oz cooked peas

50 g/2 oz hard cheese
    such as Edam or
    Cheddar, grated
fresh green salad,
    to serve

Preheat the oven to 200°C/400°F/Gas Mark 6. Scrub the potatoes dry. Prick with a fork and place on a baking sheet. Cook for 1–1½ hours or until tender when squeezed. Use oven gloves or a kitchen towel to pick up the potatoes as they will be very hot.

Cut the potatoes in half horizontally and scoop out all the flesh into a bowl. Spoon the crème fraîche into the bowl and mix thoroughly with the potatoes. Season to taste with a little salt and pepper.

Cut the ham into strips and carefully stir into the potato mixture with the broad beans, carrots and peas.

Pile the mixture back into the eight potato shells and sprinkle a little grated cheese on the top.

Place under a hot grill and cook until golden and heated through. Serve immediately with a fresh green salad.

Try This: FOR AN ALTERNATIVE: 150   FOR THE BARBECUE GRILL: 116

Beetroot & Potato Medley

SERVES 4

350 g/12 oz raw
  baby beetroot
½ tsp sunflower oil
225 g/8 oz new potatoes
½ cucumber, peeled

3 tbsp white wine vinegar
150 ml/¼ pint natural
  yogurt
salt and freshly ground
  black pepper

fresh salad leaves
1 tbsp freshly snipped
  chives, to garnish

Preheat the oven to 180°C/350°F/Gas Mark 4. Scrub the beetroot thoroughly and place on a baking tray. Brush the beetroot with a little oil and cook for 1½ hours or until a skewer is easily insertable into the beetroot. Allow to cool a little, then remove the skins.

Cook the potatoes in boiling water for about 10 minutes. Rinse in cold water and drain. Reserve the potatoes until cool. Dice evenly.

Cut the cucumber into cubes and place in a mixing bowl. Chop the beetroot into small cubes and add to the bowl with the reserved potatoes. Gently mix the vegetables together.

Mix together the vinegar and yogurt and season to taste with a little salt and pepper. Pour over the vegetables and combine gently.

Arrange on a bed of salad leaves garnished with the snipped chives and serve.

Try This: FOR AN ALTERNATIVE: 148 FOR THE BARBECUE GRILL: 48

Rice & Papaya Salad

SERVES 4

175 g/6 oz easy-cook
  basmati rice
1 cinnamon stick, bruised
1 bird's-eye chilli, deseeded
  and finely chopped
rind and juice of 2 limes
rind and juice of 2 lemons
1–2 tbsp Thai fish sauce

1 tbsp soft light brown sugar
1 papaya, peeled and
  seeds removed
1 mango, peeled and
  stone removed
1 green chilli, deseeded
  and finely chopped
2 tbsp freshly

chopped coriander
1 tbsp freshly chopped mint
250 g/9 oz cooked chicken
50 g/2 oz roasted
  peanuts, chopped
strips of pitta bread,
  to serve

Rinse and drain the rice and pour into a saucepan. Add 450 ml/¾ pint boiling salted water and the cinnamon stick. Bring to the boil, reduce the heat to a very low heat, cover and cook without stirring for 15–18 minutes, or until all the liquid is absorbed. The rice should be light and fluffy and have steam holes on the surface. Remove the cinnamon stick and stir in the rind from 1 lime.

To make the dressing, place the bird's-eye chilli, remaining rind and lime and lemon juice, fish sauce and sugar in a food processor, mix for a few minutes until blended. Alternatively, place all these ingredients in a screw-top jar and shake until well blended. Pour half the dressing over the hot rice and toss until the rice glistens.

Slice the papaya and mango into thin slices, then place in a bowl. Add the chopped green chilli, coriander and mint. Place the chicken on a chopping board, then remove and discard any skin or sinews. Cut into fine shreds and add to the bowl with the chopped peanuts.

Add the remaining dressing to the chicken mixture and stir until all the ingredients are lightly coated. Spoon the rice onto a platter, pile the chicken mixture on top and serve with warm strips of pitta bread.

Try This: FOR AN ALTERNATIVE: 196 FOR THE BARBECUE GRILL: 94

Seared Scallop Salad

SERVES 4

12 king (large) scallops
1 tbsp margarine
   or butter
2 tbsp orange juice

2 tbsp balsamic vinegar
1 tbsp clear honey
2 ripe pears, washed
125 g/4 oz rocket

125 g/4 oz watercress
50 g/2 oz walnuts
freshly ground black pepper

Clean the scallops, removing the thin black vein from around the white meat and coral. Rinse thoroughly and dry on absorbent kitchen paper. Cut into 2–3 thick slices, depending on the scallop size.

If liked, the scallops could be cooked on the barbecue – thread onto pre-soaked skewers, lightly brush with the margarine or butter and cook on a hot barbecue for 1–2 minutes turning over halfway. Or, heat a griddle pan or heavy-based frying pan, then when hot, add the margarine or butter and allow to melt. Once melted, sear the scallops for 1 minute on each side or until golden. Remove from the pan and reserve.

Briskly whisk together the orange juice, balsamic vinegar and honey to make the dressing and reserve.

With a small, sharp knife carefully cut the pears into quarters, core then cut into chunks. Mix the rocket leaves, watercress, pear chunks and walnuts.

Pile on to serving plates and top with the scallops. Drizzle over the dressing and grind over plenty of black pepper. Serve immediately.

Try This: FOR AN ALTERNATIVE: 168   FOR THE BARBECUE GRILL: 128

Smoked Mackerel & Potato Salad

SERVES 4

½ tsp dry mustard powder
1 large egg yolk
salt and freshly ground
   black pepper
150 ml/¼ pint sunflower oil
1–2 tbsp lemon juice

450 g/1 lb baby new
   potatoes
25 g/1 oz butter
350 g/12 oz smoked
   mackerel fillets
4 celery stalks, trimmed and

   finely chopped
3 tbsp creamed horseradish
150 ml/¼ pint crème fraîche
1 Little Gem lettuce, rinsed
   and roughly torn
8 cherry tomatoes, halved

Place the mustard powder and egg yolk in a small bowl with salt and pepper and whisk until blended. Add the oil, drop by drop, into the egg mixture, whisking continuously. When the mayonnaise is thick, add the lemon juice, drop by drop, until a smooth, glossy consistency is formed. Reserve.

Cook the potatoes in boiling salted water until tender, then drain. Cool slightly, then cut into halves or quarters, depending on size. Return to the saucepan and toss in the butter.

Remove the skin from the mackerel fillets and flake into pieces. Add to the potatoes in the saucepan, together with the celery.

Blend 4 tablespoons of the mayonnaise with the horseradish and crème fraîche. Season to taste with salt and pepper, then add to the potato and mackerel mixture and stir lightly.

Arrange the lettuce and tomatoes on four serving plates. Pile the smoked mackerel mixture on top of the lettuce, grind over a little pepper and serve with the remaining mayonnaise.

Try This: FOR AN ALTERNATIVE: 206   FOR THE BARBECUE GRILL: 90

Wild Rice & Bacon Salad with Smoked Chicken

SERVES 4

150 g/5 oz wild rice
50 g/2 oz pecan or
    walnut halves
1 tbsp vegetable oil
4 slices smoked
    bacon, diced

3–4 shallots, peeled and
    finely chopped
75 ml/3 fl oz walnut oil
2–3 tbsp sherry or
    cider vinegar
2 tbsp freshly chopped dill

salt and freshly ground
    black pepper
275 g/10 oz smoked
    chicken or duck
    breast, thinly sliced
dill sprigs, to garnish

Put the wild rice in a medium saucepan with 600 ml/1 pint water and bring to the boil, stirring once or twice. Reduce the heat, cover and simmer gently for 30–50 minutes, depending on the texture you prefer, chewy or tender. Using a fork, gently fluff into a large bowl and leave to cool slightly.

Meanwhile, toast the nuts in a frying pan over a medium heat for 2 minutes, or until they are fragrant and lightly coloured, stirring and tossing frequently. Cool, then chop coarsely and add to the rice.

Heat the oil in the frying pan over a medium heat. Add the bacon and cook, stirring from time to time, for 3–4 minutes, or until crisp and brown. Remove from the pan and drain on absorbent kitchen paper. Add the shallots to the pan and cook for 4 minutes, or until just softened, stirring from time to time. Stir into the rice and nuts, with the drained bacon pieces.

Whisk the walnut oil, vinegar, half the dill and salt and pepper in a small bowl until combined. Pour the dressing over the rice mixture and toss well to combine. Mix the chicken and the remaining chopped dill into the rice, then spoon into bowls and garnish each serving with a dill sprig. Serve slightly warm, or at room temperature.

Try This: FOR AN ALTERNATIVE: 160   FOR THE BARBECUE GRILL: 60

Warm Chicken & Potato Salad with Peas & Mint

SERVES 4-6

450 g/1 lb new potatoes,
  peeled or scrubbed and
  cut into bite-sized pieces
salt and freshly ground black
  pepper
2 tbsp cider vinegar
175 g/6 oz frozen garden
  peas, thawed

1 small ripe avocado
4 cooked chicken breasts,
  about 450 g/1 lb in weight,
  skinned and diced
2 tbsp freshly chopped mint
2 heads Little Gem lettuce
fresh mint sprigs, to garnish

For the dressing:
2 tbsp raspberry or
  sherry vinegar
2 tsp Dijon mustard
1 tsp clear honey
50 ml/2 fl oz sunflower oil
50 ml/2 fl oz extra virgin
  olive oil

Cook the potatoes in lightly salted boiling water for 15 minutes, or until just tender when pierced with the tip of a sharp knife; do not overcook. Rinse under cold running water to cool slightly, then drain and turn into a large bowl. Sprinkle with the cider vinegar and toss gently.

Run the peas under hot water to ensure that they are thawed, pat dry with absorbent kitchen paper and add to the potatoes.

Cut the avocado in half lengthways and remove the stone. Peel and cut the avocado into cubes and add to the potatoes and peas. Add the chicken and stir together lightly.

To make the dressing, place all the ingredients in a screw-top jar, with a little salt and pepper and shake well to mix – add a little more oil if the flavour is too sharp. Pour over the salad and toss gently to coat. Sprinkle in half the mint and stir lightly.

Separate the lettuce leaves and spread onto a large shallow serving plate. Spoon the salad on top and sprinkle with the remaining mint. Garnish with mint sprigs and serve.

Try This: FOR AN ALTERNATIVE: 152 FOR THE BARBECUE GRILL: 54

Brown Rice & Lentil Salad with Duck

SERVES 6

225 g/8 oz Puy lentils, rinsed
4 tbsp olive oil
1 medium onion, peeled and finely chopped
200 g/7 oz long-grain brown rice
½ tsp dried thyme
450 ml/¾ pint chicken stock
salt and freshly ground black pepper
350 g/12 oz shiitake or portabella mushrooms, trimmed and sliced

375 g/13 oz cooked Chinese-style spicy duck or roasted duck, sliced into chunks
2 garlic cloves, peeled and finely chopped
125 g/4 oz cooked smoked ham, diced
2 small courgettes, trimmed, diced and blanched
6 spring onions, trimmed and thinly sliced
2 tbsp freshly

chopped parsley
2 tbsp walnut halves, toasted and chopped

For the dressing:
2 tbsp red or white wine vinegar
1 tbsp balsamic vinegar
1 tsp Dijon mustard
1 tsp clear honey
75 ml/3 fl oz extra virgin olive oil
2–3 tbsp walnut oil

Bring a large saucepan of water to the boil, sprinkle in the lentils, return to the boil, then simmer over a low heat for 30 minutes, or until tender; do not overcook. Drain and rinse under cold running water, then drain again and reserve. Heat 2 tablespoons of the oil in a saucepan. Add the onion and cook for 2 minutes until it begins to soften. Stir in the rice with the thyme and stock. Season to taste with salt and pepper and bring to the boil. Cover and simmer for 40 minutes, or until tender and the liquid is absorbed.

Heat the remaining oil in a large frying pan and add the mushrooms. Cook for 5 minutes until golden. Stir in the duck and garlic and cook for 2–3 minutes to heat through. Season well.

To make the dressing, whisk the vinegars, mustard and honey in a large serving bowl, then gradually whisk in the oils. Add the lentils and the rice, then stir lightly together. Gently stir in the ham, blanched courgettes, spring onions and parsley. Season to taste and sprinkle with the walnuts. Serve topped with the duck and mushrooms.

Try This: FOR AN ALTERNATIVE: 200   FOR THE BARBECUE GRILL: 108

Bulghur Wheat Salad with Minty Lemon Dressing

SERVES 4

125 g/4 oz bulghur wheat
10 cm/4 inch piece
  cucumber
2 shallots, peeled
125 g/4 oz baby sweetcorn
3 ripe but firm tomatoes

For the dressing:
grated rind of 1 lemon
3 tbsp lemon juice
3 tbsp freshly chopped mint
2 tbsp freshly chopped
  parsley

1–2 tsp clear honey
2 tbsp sunflower oil
salt and freshly ground
  black pepper

Place the bulghur wheat in a saucepan and cover with boiling water. Simmer for about 10 minutes, then drain thoroughly and turn into a serving bowl.

Cut the cucumber into small dice, chop the shallots finely and reserve. Steam the sweetcorn over a pan of boiling water for 10 minutes or until tender. Drain and slice into thick chunks.

Cut a cross on the top of each tomato and place in boiling water until their skins start to peel away. Remove the skins and the seeds and cut the tomatoes into small dice.

Make the dressing by briskly whisking all the ingredients in a small bowl until mixed well.

When the bulghur wheat has cooled a little, add all the prepared vegetables and stir in the dressing. Season to taste with salt and pepper and serve.

Try This: FOR AN ALTERNATIVE: 170   FOR THE BARBECUE GRILL: 38

Chinese Salad with Soy & Ginger Dressing

SERVES 4

1 head of Chinese cabbage
200 g can water
   chestnuts, drained
6 spring onions, trimmed
4 ripe but firm
   cherry tomatoes
125 g/4 oz mangetout

125 g/4 oz beansprouts
2 tbsp freshly
   chopped coriander

**For the soy &
   ginger dressing:**
2 tbsp sunflower oil

4 tbsp light soy sauce
2.5 cm/1 inch piece root ginger,
   peeled and finely grated
zest and juice of 1 lemon
salt and freshly ground
   black pepper
crusty white bread, to serve

Rinse and finely shred the Chinese cabbage and place in a serving dish.

Slice the water chestnuts into small slivers and cut the spring onions diagonally into 2.5 cm/ 1 inch lengths, then split lengthwise into thin strips. Cut the tomatoes in half and then slice each half into three wedges and reserve.

Simmer the mangetout in boiling water for 2 minutes until beginning to soften, drain and cut in
half diagonally. Arrange the water chestnuts, spring onions, mangetout, tomatoes and beansprouts on top of the shredded Chinese cabbage. Garnish with the freshly chopped coriander.

Make the dressing by whisking all the ingredients together in a small bowl until mixed thoroughly. Serve with the bread and the salad.

Try This: FOR AN ALTERNATIVE: 216 FOR THE BARBECUE GRILL: 86

Curly Endive & Seafood Salad

SERVES 4

1 head of curly endive
    lettuce
2 green peppers
12.5 cm/5 inch piece
    cucumber
125 g/4 oz squid, cleaned
    and cut into thin rings
225 g/8 oz baby
    asparagus spears

125 g/4 oz smoked salmon
    slices, cut into wide strips
175 g/6 oz fresh cooked
    mussels in their shells

For the lemon dressing:
2 tbsp sunflower oil
1 tbsp white wine vinegar
5 tbsp fresh lemon juice

1–2 tsp caster sugar
1 tsp mild wholegrain
    mustard
salt and freshly ground
    black pepper

To garnish:
slices of lemon
sprigs of fresh coriander

Rinse and tear the endive into small pieces and arrange on a serving platter. Remove the seeds from the peppers and cut the peppers and the cucumber into small dice. Sprinkle over the endive.

Bring a saucepan of water to the boil and add the squid rings. Bring the pan up to the boil again, then switch off the heat and leave it to stand for 5 minutes. Then drain and rinse thoroughly in cold water.

Cook the asparagus in boiling water for 5 minutes or until tender but just crisp. Arrange with the squid, smoked salmon and mussels on top of the salad.

To make the lemon dressing, put all the ingredients into a screw-topped jar or into a small bowl and mix thoroughly until the ingredients are combined.

Spoon 3 tablespoons of the dressing over the salad and serve the remainder in a small jug. Garnish the salad with slices of lemon and sprigs of coriander and serve.

Try This: FOR AN ALTERNATIVE: 154   FOR THE BARBECUE GRILL: 80

Warm Fruity Rice Salad

SERVES 4

175 g/6 oz mixed basmati
and wild rice
125 g/4 oz skinless
chicken breast
300 ml/½ pint chicken or
vegetable stock
125 g/4 oz ready-to-eat
dried apricots

125 g/4 oz ready-to-eat
dried dates
3 sticks celery

For the dressing:
2 tbsp sunflower oil
1 tbsp white wine vinegar
4 tbsp lemon juice

1–2 tsp clear honey, warmed
1 tsp Dijon mustard
freshly ground black pepper

To garnish:
6 spring onions
sprigs of fresh coriander

Place the rice in a pan of boiling salted water and cook for 15–20 minutes or until tender. Rinse thoroughly with boiling water and reserve.

Meanwhile wipe the chicken and place in a shallow saucepan with the stock. Bring to the boil, cover and simmer for about 15 minutes or until the chicken is cooked thoroughly and the juices run clear. Leave the chicken in the stock until cool enough to handle, then cut into thin slices.

Chop the apricots and dates into small pieces. Peel any tough membranes from the outside of the celery and chop into dice. Fold the apricots, dates, celery and sliced chicken into the warm rice.

Make the dressing by whisking all the ingredients together in a small bowl until mixed thoroughly. Pour 2–3 tablespoons over the rice and stir in gently and evenly. Serve the remaining dressing separately.

Trim and chop the spring onions. Sprinkle the spring onions over the top of the salad and garnish with the sprigs of coriander. Serve while still warm.

Try This: FOR AN ALTERNATIVE: 152   FOR THE BARBECUE GRILL: 68

Warm Leek & Tomato Salad

SERVES 4

450 g/1 lb trimmed
   baby leeks
225 g/8 oz ripe, but
   firm tomatoes
2 shallots, peeled and cut
   into thin wedges

For the dressing:
2 tbsp clear honey
grated rind of 1 lime
4 tbsp lime juice
1 tbsp light olive oil
1 tsp Dijon mustard

salt and freshly ground
   black pepper

To garnish:
freshly chopped tarragon
freshly chopped basil

Trim the leeks so that they are all the same length. Place in a steamer over a pan of boiling water and steam for 8 minutes or until just tender. Drain the leeks thoroughly and arrange in a shallow serving dish.

Make a cross in the top of the tomatoes, place in a bowl and cover them with boiling water until their skins start to peel away. Remove from the bowl and carefully remove the skins.

Cut the tomatoes into four and remove the seeds, then chop into small dice.
Spoon over the top of the leeks together with the shallots.

In a small bowl make the dressing by whisking the honey, lime rind, lime juice, olive oil, mustard and salt and pepper. Pour 3 tablespoons of the dressing over the leeks and tomatoes and garnish with the tarragon and basil. Serve while the leeks are still warm, with the remaining dressing served separately.

Try This: FOR AN ALTERNATIVE: 204 FOR THE BARBECUE GRILL: 26

Mediterranean Feast

SERVES 4

1 small iceberg lettuce
225 g/8 oz baby new
    potatoes, scrubbed
225 g/8 oz French beans
4 medium eggs
1 green pepper
1 medium onion, peeled
200 g can tuna in brine,
    drained and flaked into
    small pieces

50 g/2 oz hard cheese,
    such as Edam, cut
    into small cubes
8 ripe but firm cherry
    tomatoes, quartered
50 g/2 oz black pitted
    olives, halved
freshly chopped basil,
    to garnish

For the lime vinaigrette:
3 tbsp light olive oil
2 tbsp white wine vinegar
4 tbsp lime juice
grated rind of 1 lime
1 tsp Dijon mustard
1-2 tsp caster sugar
salt and freshly ground
    black pepper

Cut the lettuce into four and remove the hard core. Tear into bite-sized pieces and arrange on a large serving platter or four individual plates. Cook the potatoes in boiling salted water for 15–20 minutes or until tender, and the French beans for 8 minutes. Drain and rinse in cold water until cool, then cut both the beans and potatoes in half with a sharp knife.

Boil the eggs for 10 minutes, then rinse thoroughly under a cold running tap until cool. Remove the shells under water and cut each egg into four. Remove the seeds from the pepper and cut into thin strips and finely chop the onion.

Arrange the beans, potatoes, eggs, peppers and onion on top of the lettuce. Add the tuna, cheese and tomatoes. Sprinkle over the olives and garnish with the basil.

To make the vinaigrette, place all the ingredients in a screw-topped jar and shake vigorously until everything is mixed thoroughly. Spoon 4 tablespoons over the top of the prepared salad and serve the remainder separately.

Try This: FOR AN ALTERNATIVE: 206   FOR THE BARBECUE GRILL: 42

Carrot, Celeriac & Sesame Seed Salad

SERVES 6

225 g/8 oz celeriac
225 g/8 oz carrots, peeled
50 g/2 oz seedless raisins
2 tbsp sesame seeds
freshly chopped parsley,
   to garnish

**For the lemon &
   chilli dressing:**
grated rind of 1 lemon
4 tbsp lemon juice
2 tbsp sunflower oil
2 tbsp clear honey

1 red bird's eye
   chilli, deseeded and
   finely chopped
salt and freshly ground
   black pepper

Slice the celeriac into thin matchsticks. Place in a small saucepan of boiling salted water and boil for 2 minutes.

Drain and rinse the celeriac in cold water and place in a mixing bowl. Finely grate the carrot. Add the carrot and the raisins to the celeriac in the bowl.

Place the sesame seeds under a hot grill or dry-fry in a frying pan for 1–2 minutes until golden brown, then leave to cool.

Make the dressing by whisking together the lemon rind, lemon juice, oil, honey, chilli and seasoning or by shaking thoroughly in a screw-topped jar.

Pour 2 tablespoons of the dressing over the salad and toss well. Turn into a serving dish and sprinkle over the toasted sesame seeds and chopped parsley. Serve the remaining dressing separately.

Try This: FOR AN ALTERNATIVE: 146 FOR THE BARBECUE GRILL: 34

Indonesian Salad with Peanut Dressing

SERVES 4

225 g/8 oz new potatoes, scrubbed
1 large carrot, peeled and cut into matchsticks
125 g/4 oz French beans, trimmed
225 g/8 oz tiny cauliflower florets
125 g/4 oz cucumber, cut into matchsticks
75 g/3 oz fresh bean sprouts
3 medium eggs, hard-boiled and quartered

For the peanut dressing:
2 tbsp sesame oil
1 garlic clove, peeled and crushed
1 red chilli, deseeded and finely chopped
150 g/5 oz crunchy peanut butter
6 tbsp hot vegetable stock
2 tsp soft light brown sugar
2 tsp dark soy sauce
1 tbsp lime juice

Cook the potatoes in a saucepan of boiling salted water for 15–20 minutes until tender. Remove with a slotted spoon and thickly slice into a large bowl. Keep the saucepan of water boiling.

Add the carrot, French beans and cauliflower to the water, return to the boil and cook for 2 minutes, or until just tender. Drain and refresh under cold running water, then drain well. Add to the potatoes with the cucumber and bean sprouts.

To make the dressing, gently heat the sesame oil in a small saucepan. Add the garlic and chilli and cook for a few seconds, then remove from the heat. Stir in the peanut butter.

Stir in the stock, a little at a time. Add the remaining ingredients and mix together to make a thick, creamy dressing.

Divide the vegetables between four plates and arrange the eggs on top. Drizzle the dressing over the salad and serve immediately.

Try This: FOR AN ALTERNATIVE: 220   FOR THE BARBECUE GRILL: 110

Baby Roast Potato Salad

SERVES 4

350 g/12 oz small shallots
sea salt and freshly ground
    black pepper
900 g/2 lb small even-sized
    new potatoes

2 tbsp olive oil
2 medium courgettes
2 sprigs of fresh rosemary
175 g/6 oz cherry tomatoes
150 ml/¼ pint soured cream

2 tbsp freshly
    snipped chives
¼ tsp paprika

Preheat the oven to 200°C/400°F/Gas Mark 6. Trim the shallots, but leave the skins on. Put in a saucepan of lightly salted boiling water with the potatoes and cook for 5 minutes, then drain. Separate the shallots and plunge them into cold water for 1 minute.

Put the oil in a baking sheet lined with tinfoil or roasting tin and heat for a few minutes. Peel the skins off the shallots – they should now come away easily. Add to the baking sheet or roasting tin with the potatoes and toss in the oil to coat. Sprinkle with a little sea salt. Roast the potatoes and shallots in the preheated oven for 10 minutes.

Meanwhile, trim the courgettes, halve lengthways and cut into 5 cm/2 inch chunks. Add to the baking sheet or roasting tin, toss to mix and cook for 5 minutes.

Pierce the tomato skins with a sharp knife. Add to the sheet or tin with the rosemary and cook for a further 5 minutes, or until all the vegetables are tender. Remove the rosemary and discard. Grind a little black pepper over the vegetables.

Spoon into a wide serving bowl. Mix together the soured cream and chives and drizzle over the vegetables just before serving.

Try This: FOR AN ALTERNATIVE: 160 FOR THE BARBECUE GRILL: 88

Mediterranean Rice Salad

SERVES 4

250 g/9 oz Camargue
   red rice
2 sun-dried tomatoes,
   finely chopped
2 garlic cloves, peeled
   and finely chopped
4 tbsp oil from a jar of
   sun-dried tomatoes (or
   olive oil)

2 tsp balsamic vinegar
2 tsp red wine vinegar
salt and freshly ground
   black pepper
1 red onion, peeled and
   thinly sliced
1 yellow pepper, quartered
   and deseeded
1 red pepper, quartered

   and deseeded
½ cucumber,
   peeled and diced
6 ripe plum tomatoes,
   cut into wedges
1 fennel bulb, halved
   and thinly sliced
fresh basil leaves,
   to garnish

Cook the rice in a saucepan of lightly salted boiling water for 35–40 minutes, or until tender. Drain well and reserve.

Whisk the sun-dried tomatoes, garlic, oil and vinegars together in a small bowl or jug. Season to taste with salt and pepper. Put the red onion in a large bowl, pour over the dressing and leave to allow the flavours to develop.

Put the peppers skin-side up on a grill rack and cook under a preheated hot grill for 5–6 minutes, or until blackened and charred. Remove and place in a plastic bag. When cool enough to handle, peel off the skins and slice the peppers.

Add the peppers, cucumber, tomatoes, fennel and rice to the onions. Mix gently together to coat in the dressing. Cover and chill in the refrigerator for 30 minutes to allow the flavours to mingle.

Remove the salad from the refrigerator and leave to stand at room temperature for 20 minutes. Garnish with fresh basil leaves and serve.

Try This: FOR AN ALTERNATIVE: 184   FOR THE BARBECUE GRILL: 62

Chef's Rice Salad

SERVES 4

225 g/8 oz wild rice
1/2 cucumber
175 g/6 oz cherry tomatoes
6 spring onions, trimmed
5 tbsp extra virgin olive oil
2 tbsp balsamic vinegar
1 tsp Dijon mustard

1 tsp caster sugar
salt and freshly ground
black pepper
125 g/4 oz rocket
125 g/4 oz back bacon
125 g/4 oz cooked chicken
meat, finely diced

125 g/4 oz Emmenthal
cheese, grated
125 g/4 oz large cooked
prawns, peeled
1 avocado, stoned, peeled
and sliced, to garnish
warm crusty bread, to serve

Put the rice in in a saucepan of water and bring to the boil, stirring once or twice. Reduce the heat, cover and simmer gently for 30–50 minutes, depending on the texture you prefer. Drain well and reserve.

Thinly peel the cucumber, cut in half, then using a teaspoon, remove the seeds. Cut the cucumber into thin slices. Cut the tomatoes in quarters. Cut the spring onions into diagonal slices.

Whisk the olive oil with the vinegar, then whisk in the mustard and sugar. Season to taste with salt and pepper.

In a large bowl, gently toss together the cooled rice with the tomatoes, cucumber, spring onions and the rocket. Pour over the dressing and toss lightly together.

Heat a griddle pan and when hot cook the bacon on both sides for 4–6 minutes, or until crisp. Remove and chop. Arrange the prepared rocket salad on a platter, then arrange the bacon, chicken, cheese and prawns on top. Toss, if wished. Garnish with avocado slices and serve with plenty of warm, crusty bread.

Try This: FOR AN ALTERNATIVE: 182   FOR THE BARBECUE GRILL: 36

Warm Potato, Pear & Pecan Salad

SERVES 4

900 g/2 lb new potatoes, preferably red-skinned, unpeeled	1 tsp Dijon mustard	2 firm ripe dessert pears
	2 tsp white wine vinegar	2 tsp lemon juice
	3 tbsp groundnut oil	175 g/6 oz baby spinach leaves
salt and freshly ground black pepper	1 tbsp hazelnut or walnut oil	
	2 tsp poppy seeds	75 g/3 oz toasted pecan nuts

Scrub the potatoes, then cook in a saucepan of lightly salted boiling water for 15 minutes, or until tender. Drain, cut into halves, or quarters if large, and place in a serving bowl.

In a small bowl or jug, whisk together the mustard and vinegar. Gradually add the oils until the mixture begins to thicken. Stir in the poppy seeds and season to taste with salt and pepper.

Pour about two thirds of the dressing over the hot potatoes and toss gently to coat. Leave until the potatoes have soaked up the dressing and are just warm.

Meanwhile, quarter and core the pears. Cut into thin slices, then sprinkle with the lemon juice to prevent them from going brown. Add to the potatoes with the spinach leaves and toasted pecan nuts. Gently mix together.

Drizzle the remaining dressing over the salad. Serve immediately before the spinach starts to wilt.

Try This: FOR AN ALTERNATIVE: 160   FOR THE BARBECUE GRILL: 70

Mediterranean Potato Salad

SERVES 4

700 g/1½ lb small
  waxy potatoes
2 red onions, peeled and
  roughly chopped
1 yellow pepper, deseeded
  and roughly chopped
1 green pepper, deseeded
  and roughly chopped

6 tbsp extra virgin olive oil
125 g/4 oz ripe tomatoes,
  chopped
50 g/2 oz pitted black
  olives, sliced
125 g/4 oz feta cheese
3 tbsp freshly chopped
  parsley

2 tbsp white wine vinegar
1 tsp Dijon mustard
1 tsp clear honey
salt and freshly ground
  black pepper
sprigs of fresh parsley,
  to garnish

Preheat the oven to 200°C/400°F/Gas Mark 6. Place the potatoes in a large saucepan of salted water, bring to the boil and simmer until just tender. Do not overcook. Drain and plunge into cold water, to stop them from cooking further.

Meanwhile, place the onions in a bowl with the yellow and green peppers, then pour over 2 tablespoons of the olive oil. Stir and spoon onto a large baking tray. Cook in the preheated oven for 25–30 minutes, or until the vegetables are tender and lightly charred in places, stirring occasionally. Remove from the oven and transfer to a large bowl.

Cut the potatoes into bite-sized pieces and mix with the roasted onions and peppers. Add the tomatoes and olives to the potatoes. Crumble over the feta cheese and sprinkle with the chopped parsley.

Whisk together the remaining olive oil, vinegar, mustard and honey, then season to taste with salt and pepper. Pour the dressing over the potatoes and toss gently together. Garnish with parsley sprigs and serve immediately.

Try This: FOR AN ALTERNATIVE: 186   FOR THE BARBECUE GRILL: 54

Mixed Salad with Anchovy Dressing & Ciabatta Croûtons

SERVES 4

1 small head endive
1 small head chicory
1 fennel bulb
400 g can artichokes,
    drained and rinsed
½ cucumber
125 g/4 oz cherry tomatoes

75 g/3 oz black olives

For the anchovy dressing:
50 g can anchovy fillets
1 tsp Dijon mustard
1 small garlic clove, peeled
    and crushed

4 tbsp olive oil
1 tbsp lemon juice
freshly ground black pepper

For the ciabatta croûtons:
2 thick slices ciabatta bread
2 tbsp olive oil

Divide the endive and chicory into leaves and reserve some of the larger ones. Arrange the smaller leaves in a wide salad bowl.

Cut the fennel bulb in half from the stalk to the root end, then cut across in fine slices. Quarter the artichokes, then quarter and slice the cucumber and halve the tomatoes. Add to the salad bowl with the olives.

To make the dressing, drain the anchovies and put in a blender with the mustard, garlic, olive oil, lemon juice, 2 tablespoons of hot water and black pepper. Whiz together until smooth and thickened.

To make the croûtons, cut the bread into 1 cm/½ inch cubes. Heat the oil in a frying pan, add the bread cubes and fry for 3 minutes, turning frequently until golden. Remove and drain on absorbent kitchen paper.

Drizzle half the anchovy dressing over the prepared salad and toss to coat. Arrange the reserved endive and chicory leaves around the edge, then drizzle over the remaining dressing. Scatter over the croûtons and serve immediately.

Try This: FOR AN ALTERNATIVE: 188   FOR THE BARBECUE GRILL: 104

Panzanella

SERVES 4

250 g/9 oz day-old Italian-
    style bread
1 tbsp red wine vinegar
4 tbsp olive oil
1 tsp lemon juice
1 small garlic clove, peeled
    and finely chopped

1 red onion, peeled and
    finely sliced
1 cucumber, peeled
    if preferred
225 g/8 oz ripe tomatoes,
    deseeded
150 g/5 oz pitted black olives

about 20 basil leaves,
    coarsely torn or left
    whole if small
sea salt and freshly ground
    black pepper

Cut the bread into thick slices, leaving the crusts on. Add 1 teaspoon of red wine vinegar to a jug of iced water, put the slices of bread in a bowl and pour over the water. Make sure the bread is covered completely. Leave to soak for 3–4 minutes until just soft.

Remove the soaked bread from the water and squeeze it gently, first with your hands and then in a clean tea towel to remove any excess water. Put the bread on a plate, cover with clingfilm and chill in the refrigerator for about 1 hour.

Meanwhile, whisk together the olive oil, the remaining red wine vinegar and lemon juice in a large serving bowl. Add the garlic and onion and stir to coat well.

Halve the cucumber and remove the seeds. Chop both the cucumber and tomatoes into 1 cm/½ inch dice. Add to the garlic and onions with the olives. Tear the bread into bite-sized chunks and add to the bowl with the fresh basil leaves. Toss together to mix and serve immediately, with a grinding of sea salt and black pepper.

    Try This: FOR AN ALTERNATIVE: 190   FOR THE BARBECUE GRILL: 46

Tortellini & Summer Vegetable Salad

SERVES 6

350 g/12 oz mixed green and plain cheese-filled fresh tortellini
150 ml/¼ pint extra virgin olive oil
225 g/8 oz fine green beans, trimmed
175 g/6 oz broccoli florets
1 yellow or red pepper, deseeded and thinly sliced
1 red onion, peeled and sliced
175 g jar marinated artichoke hearts, drained and halved
2 tbsp capers
75 g/3 oz dry-cured pitted black olives
3 tbsp raspberry or balsamic vinegar
1 tbsp Dijon mustard
1 tsp soft brown sugar
salt and freshly ground black pepper
2 tbsp freshly chopped basil or flat leaf parsley
2 quartered hard-boiled eggs, to garnish

Bring a large pan of lightly salted water to a rolling boil. Add the tortellini and cook according to the packet instructions, or until 'al dente'.

Using a large slotted spoon, transfer the tortellini to a colander to drain. Rinse under cold running water and drain again. Transfer to a large bowl and toss with 2 tablespoons of the olive oil.

Return the pasta water to the boil and drop in the green beans and broccoli florets; blanch them for 2 minutes, or until just beginning to soften. Drain, rinse under cold running water and drain again thoroughly. Add the vegetables to the reserved tortellini. Add the pepper, onion, artichoke hearts, capers and olives to the bowl; stir lightly.

Whisk together the vinegar, mustard and brown sugar in a bowl and season to taste with salt and pepper. Slowly whisk in the remaining olive oil to form a thick, creamy dressing. Pour over the tortellini and vegetables, add the chopped basil or parsley and stir until lightly coated. Transfer to a shallow serving dish or salad bowl. Garnish with the hard-boiled egg quarters and serve.

Try This: FOR AN ALTERNATIVE: 220 FOR THE BARBECUE GRILL: 106

Chicken & Pasta Salad

SERVES 6

450 g/1 lb short pasta
2–3 tbsp extra virgin olive oil
300 g/11 oz cold cooked
   chicken, cut into bite-sized
   pieces (preferably roasted)
1 red pepper, deseeded
   and diced
1 yellow pepper,
   deseeded and diced
4–5 sun-dried tomatoes,

sliced
2 tbsp capers, rinsed
   and drained
125 g/4 oz pitted Italian
   black olives
4 spring onions, chopped
225 g/8 oz mozzarella
   cheese, preferably
   buffalo, diced
salt and freshly ground

black pepper

For the dressing:
50 ml/2 fl oz red or white
   wine vinegar
1 tbsp mild mustard
1 tsp sugar
75–125 ml/ 3–4 fl oz
   extra virgin olive oil
125 ml/4 fl oz mayonnaise

Bring a large saucepan of lightly salted water to the boil. Add the pasta and cook for 10 minutes, or until 'al dente'. Drain the pasta and rinse under cold running water, then drain again. Place in a large serving bowl and toss with the olive oil.

Add the chicken, diced red and yellow peppers, sliced sun-dried tomatoes, capers, olives, spring onions and mozzarella to the pasta and toss gently until mixed. Season to taste with salt and pepper.

To make the dressing, put the vinegar, mustard and sugar into a small bowl or jug and whisk until well blended and the sugar is dissolved. Season with some pepper, then gradually whisk in the olive oil in a slow, steady stream until a thickened vinaigrette forms.

Put the mayonnaise in a bowl and gradually whisk in the dressing until smooth. Pour over the pasta mixture and mix gently until all the ingredients are coated. Turn into a large, shallow serving bowl and serve at room temperature.

Try This: FOR AN ALTERNATIVE: 200   FOR THE BARBECUE GRILL: 54

Turkey & Oven–roasted Vegetable Salad

SERVES 4

6 tbsp olive oil
3 medium courgettes, trimmed and sliced
2 yellow peppers, deseeded and sliced
125 g/4 oz pine nuts
275 g/10 oz macaroni

350 g/12 oz cooked turkey
280 g jar or can chargrilled artichokes, drained and sliced
225 g/8 oz baby plum tomatoes, quartered
4 tbsp freshly chopped

coriander
1 garlic clove, peeled and chopped
3 tbsp balsamic vinegar
salt and freshly ground black pepper

Preheat the oven to 200°C/400°F/Gas Mark 6, 15 minutes before cooking. Line a large roasting tin with tinfoil, pour in half the olive oil and place in the oven for 3 minutes, or until very hot. Remove from the oven, add the courgettes and peppers and stir until evenly coated. Bake for 30–35 minutes, or until slightly charred, turning occasionally.

Add the pine nuts to the tin. Return to the oven and bake for 10 minutes, or until the pine nuts are toasted. Remove from the oven and allow the vegetables to cool completely.

Bring a large pan of lightly salted water to a rolling boil. Add the macaroni and cook according to the packet instructions, or until 'al dente'. Drain and refresh under cold running water then drain thoroughly and place in a large salad bowl.

Cut the turkey into bite-sized pieces and add to the macaroni. Add the artichokes and tomatoes with the cooled vegetables and pan juices to the pan. Blend together the coriander, garlic, remaining oil, vinegar and seasoning. Pour over the salad, toss lightly and serve.

Try This: FOR AN ALTERNATIVE: 196   FOR THE BARBECUE GRILL: 120

Hot Duck Pasta Salad

SERVES 6

3 boneless and skinless
    duck breasts
1 tbsp wholegrain mustard
1 tbsp clear honey
salt and freshly ground
    black pepper
4 medium eggs

450 g/1 lb fusilli
125 g/4 oz French
    beans, trimmed
1 large carrot, peeled and
    cut into thin batons
125 g/4 oz sweetcorn
    kernels, cooked if frozen

75 g/3 oz fresh baby spinach
    leaves, shredded

For the dressing:
8 tbsp French dressing
1 tsp horseradish sauce
4 tbsp crème fraîche

Preheat the oven to 200°C/400°F/Gas Mark 6. Place the duck breasts on a baking tray lined with tinfoil. Mix together the wholegrain mustard and honey, season lightly with salt and pepper then spread over the duck breasts. Roast in the preheated oven for 20–30 minutes, or until tender. Remove from the oven and keep warm.

Meanwhile, place the eggs in a small saucepan, cover with water and bring to the boil. Simmer for 8 minutes, then drain. Bring a large pan of lightly salted water to a rolling boil. Add the beans and pasta, return to the boil and cook according to the packet instructions, or until 'al dente'. Drain the pasta and beans and refresh under cold running water.

Place the pasta and beans in a bowl, add the carrot, sweetcorn and spinach leaves and toss lightly. Shell the eggs, cut into wedges and arrange on top of the pasta. Slice the duck breasts then place them on top of the salad. Beat the dressing ingredients together in a bowl until well blended, then drizzle over the salad. Serve immediately.

Pasta & Pepper Salad

SERVES 4

4 tbsp olive oil
1 each red, orange
   and yellow pepper,
   deseeded and cut
   into chunks
1 large courgette, trimmed
   and cut into chunks
1 medium aubergine,
   trimmed and diced

275 g/10 oz fusilli
4 plum tomatoes, quartered
1 bunch fresh basil leaves,
   roughly chopped
2 tbsp pesto
2 garlic cloves, peeled and
   roughly chopped
1 tbsp lemon juice
225 g/8 oz boneless and

   skinless roasted
   chicken breast
salt and freshly ground
   black pepper
125 g/4 oz feta cheese,
   crumbled
crusty bread, to serve

Preheat the oven to 200°C/400°F/Gas Mark 6. Spoon the olive oil into a roasting tin and heat in the oven for 2 minutes, or until almost smoking. Remove from the oven, add the peppers, courgette and aubergine and stir until coated. Bake for 30 minutes, or until charred, stirring occasionally.

Bring a large pan of lightly salted water to a rolling boil. Add the pasta and cook according to the packet instructions, or until 'al dente'. Drain and refresh under cold running water. Drain thoroughly, place in a large salad bowl and reserve.

Remove the cooked vegetables from the oven and allow to cool. Add to the cooled pasta, together with the quartered tomatoes, chopped basil leaves, pesto, garlic and lemon juice. Toss lightly to mix.

Shred the chicken roughly into small pieces and stir into the pasta and vegetable mixture. Season to taste with salt and pepper, then sprinkle the crumbled feta cheese over the pasta and stir gently. Cover the dish and leave to marinate for 30 minutes, stirring occasionally. Serve the salad with fresh crusty bread.

Try This: FOR AN ALTERNATIVE: 144   FOR THE BARBECUE GRILL: 92

Marinated Mackerel with Tomato & Basil Salad

SERVES 3

3 mackerel, filleted
3 beefsteak tomatoes, sliced
50 g/2 oz watercress
2 oranges, peeled and
    segmented
75 g/3 oz mozzarella
    cheese, sliced
2 tbsp basil leaves, shredded

sprig of fresh basil,
    to garnish

For the marinade:
juice of 2 lemons
4 tbsp olive oil
4 tbsp basil leaves

For the dressing:
1 tbsp lemon juice
1 tsp Dijon mustard
1 tsp caster sugar
salt and freshly ground
    black pepper
5 tbsp olive oil

Remove as many of the fine pin bones as possible from the mackerel fillets, lightly rinse and pat dry with absorbent kitchen paper and place in a shallow dish.

Blend the marinade ingredients together and pour over the mackerel fillets. Make sure the marinade has covered the fish completely. Cover and leave in a refrigerator for at least 8 hours, but preferably overnight. As the fillets marinate, they will loose their translucency and look as if they are cooked.

Place the tomatoes, watercress, oranges and mozzarella cheese in a large bowl and toss. To make the dressing, whisk the lemon juice with the mustard, sugar and seasoning in a bowl. Pour over half the dressing, toss again and then arrange on a serving platter.

Remove the mackerel from the marinade, cut into bite-sized pieces and sprinkle with the shredded basil. Arrange on top of the salad, drizzle over the remaining dressing, scatter with basil leaves and garnish with a basil sprig. Serve.

Try This: FOR AN ALTERNATIVE: 206   FOR THE BARBECUE GRILL: 72

Fresh Tuna Salad

SERVES 4

225 g/8 oz mixed
    salad leaves
225 g/8 oz baby cherry
    tomatoes, halved
    lengthways
125 g/4 oz rocket
    leaves, washed

2 tbsp groundnut oil
4 tuna steaks, each cut into 4
    pieces, about 550 g/1¼ lb
    total weight
50 g/2 oz piece fresh
    Parmesan cheese

For the dressing:
8 tbsp olive oil
grated zest and juice of
    2 small lemons
1 tbsp wholegrain mustard
salt and freshly ground
    black pepper

Wash the salad leaves and place in a large salad bowl with the cherry tomatoes and rocket and reserve.

Heat the wok, then add the oil and heat until almost smoking. Add the tuna, skin-side down, and cook for 4–6 minutes, turning once during cooking, or until cooked and the flesh flakes easily. Remove from the heat and leave to stand in the juices for 2 minutes before removing.

Meanwhile make the dressing, place the olive oil, lemon zest and juices and mustard in a small bowl or screw-topped jar and whisk or shake well until well blended. Season to taste with salt and pepper.

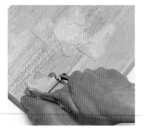

Transfer the tuna to a clean chopping board and flake, then add it to the salad and toss lightly.

Using a swivel blade vegetable peeler, peel the piece of Parmesan cheese into shavings. Divide the salad between four large serving plates, drizzle the dressing over the salad, then scatter with the Parmesan shavings.

Try This: FOR AN ALTERNATIVE: 174   FOR THE BARBECUE GRILL: 92

Prawn Salad
with Toasted Rice

SERVES 4

For the dressing:
50 ml/2 fl oz rice vinegar
1 red chilli, deseeded and
   thinly sliced
7.5 cm/3 inch piece lemon
   grass stalk, bruised
juice of 1 lime
1–2 tbsp Thai fish sauce
1 tsp sugar, or to taste

For the salad:
350 g/12 oz large raw
   prawns, peeled with tails
   attached, heads removed
cayenne pepper
1 tbsp long-grain white rice
salt and freshly ground
   black pepper
2 tbsp sunflower oil

1 large head Chinese leaves
   or cos lettuce, shredded
½ small cucumber,
   peeled, deseeded and
   thinly sliced
1 small bunch chives, cut
   into 2.5 cm/1 inch pieces
small bunch of mint leaves

Place all the ingredients for the dressing in a small bowl and leave to stand to let the flavours blend together.

Using a sharp knife, split each prawn lengthways in half, leaving the tail attached to one half. Remove any black vein and pat the prawns dry with absorbent kitchen paper. Sprinkle the prawns with a little salt and cayenne pepper and then reserve.

Heat a wok over a high heat. Add the rice and stir-fry until browned and fragrant. Turn into a mortar and cool. Crush gently with a pestle until coarse crumbs form. Wipe the wok clean.

Reheat the wok, add the oil and when hot, add the prawns and stir-fry for 2 minutes, or until pink. Transfer to a plate and season to taste with salt and pepper.

Place the Chinese leaves or lettuce into a salad bowl with the cucumber, chives and mint leaves and toss lightly together. Remove the lemon grass stalk and some of the chilli from the dressing and pour all but 2 tablespoons over the salad and toss until lightly coated. Add the prawns and drizzle with the remaining dressing, then sprinkle with the toasted rice and serve.

Try This: FOR AN ALTERNATIVE: 210 FOR THE BARBECUE GRILL: 110

Thai Prawn & Rice Noodle Salad

SERVES 4

75 g/3 oz rice vermicelli
175 g/6 oz mangetout, cut in half crossways
½ cucumber, peeled, deseeded and diced
2–3 spring onions, trimmed and thinly sliced diagonally
16–20 large cooked tiger prawns, peeled with tails left on
2 tbsp chopped unsalted peanuts or cashews

For the dressing:
4 tbsp freshly squeezed lime juice
2–3 tbsp Thai fish sauce
1 tbsp sugar
2.5 cm/1 inch piece fresh root ginger, peeled and finely chopped
1 red chilli, deseeded and thinly sliced
3–4 tbsp freshly chopped coriander or mint

To garnish:
lime wedges
sprigs of fresh mint

Place the vermicelli in a bowl and pour over hot water to cover. Leave to stand for 5 minutes or until softened. Drain, rinse, then drain again and reserve.

Meanwhile, mix all the dressing ingredients in a large bowl until well blended and the sugar has dissolved. Reserve.

Bring a medium saucepan of water to the boil. Add the mangetout, return to the boil and cook for 30–50 seconds. Drain, refresh under cold running water, drain again and reserve.

Stir the cucumber, spring onions and all but 4 of the prawns into the dressing until coated lightly. Add the mangetout and noodles and toss until all the ingredients are mixed evenly.

Spoon the noodle salad on to warmed individual plates. Sprinkle with peanuts or cashews and garnish each dish with a reserved prawn, a lime wedge and a sprig of mint.

Try This: FOR AN ALTERNATIVE: 208   FOR THE BARBECUE GRILL: 98

Warm Lobster Salad with Hot Thai Dressing

SERVES 4

1 orange
50 g/2 oz granulated sugar
2 Cos lettuce hearts, shredded
1 small avocado, peeled and thinly sliced
½ cucumber, peeled, deseeded and thinly sliced
1 ripe mango, peeled, stoned and thinly sliced
1 tbsp butter or vegetable oil
1 large lobster, meat

removed and cut into bite-sized pieces
2 tbsp Thai or Italian basil leaves
4 large cooked prawns, peeled with tails left on, to garnish

For the dressing:
1 tbsp vegetable oil
4–6 spring onions, trimmed and sliced diagonally into 5 cm/2 inch pieces

2.5 cm/1 inch piece fresh root ginger, peeled and grated
1 garlic clove, peeled and crushed
grated zest of 1 lime
juice of 2–3 small limes
1–2 tbsp Thai fish sauce
1 tbsp brown sugar
1–2 tsp sweet chilli sauce, or to taste
1 tbsp sesame oil

With a sharp knife, cut the orange rind into thin julienne strips, then cook in boiling water for 2 minutes. Drain the orange strips, then plunge into cold running water, drain and return to the saucepan with the sugar and 1 cm/½ inch water. Simmer until soft, then add 1 tablespoon of cold water to stop cooking. Remove from the heat and reserve. Arrange the lettuce on four large plates and arrange the avocado, cucumber and mango slices over the lettuce.

Heat a wok or large frying pan, add the butter or oil and when hot, but not sizzling, add the lobster and stir-fry for 1–2 minutes or until heated through. Remove and drain on absorbent kitchen paper. To make the dressing, heat the vegetable oil in a wok, then add the spring onions, ginger and garlic and stir-fry for 1 minute. Add the lime zest, lime juice, fish sauce, sugar and chilli sauce. Stir until the sugar dissolves. Remove from the heat, add the sesame oil with the orange rind and liquor. Arrange the lobster meat over the salad and drizzle with dressing. Sprinkle with basil leaves, garnish with prawns and serve immediately.

Try This: FOR AN ALTERNATIVE: 210   FOR THE BARBECUE GRILL: 94

Chicken Satay Salad

SERVES 4

4 tbsp crunchy peanut butter
1 tbsp chilli sauce
1 garlic clove, peeled
   and crushed
2 tbsp cider vinegar
2 tbsp light soy sauce
2 tbsp dark soy sauce

2 tsp soft brown sugar
pinch of salt
2 tsp freshly ground
   Szechuan peppercorns
450 g/1 lb dried egg noodles
2 tbsp sesame oil
1 tbsp groundnut oil

450 g/1 lb skinless, boneless
   chicken breast fillets, cut
   into cubes
shredded celery leaves,
   to garnish
cos lettuce, to serve

Place the peanut butter, chilli sauce, garlic, cider vinegar, soy sauces, sugar, salt and ground peppercorns in a food processor and blend to form a smooth paste. Scrape into a bowl, cover and chill in the refrigerator until required.

Bring a large saucepan of lightly salted water to the boil. Add the noodles and cook for 3–5 minutes. Drain and plunge into cold water. Drain again and toss in the sesame oil. Leave to cool.

Heat the wok until very hot, add the oil and when hot, add the chicken cubes. Stir-fry for 5–6 minutes until the chicken is golden brown and cooked through.

Remove the chicken from the wok using a slotted spoon and add to the noodles, together with the peanut sauce. Mix lightly together, then sprinkle with the shredded celery leaves and either serve immediately or leave until cold, then serve with cos lettuce.

Try This: FOR AN ALTERNATIVE: 220   FOR THE BARBECUE GRILL: 124

Oriental Noodle & Peanut Salad with Coriander

SERVES 4

350 g/12 oz rice vermicelli
1 litre/1¾ pints light
  vegetable stock
2 tsp sesame oil
2 tbsp light soy sauce
8 spring onions

3 tbsp groundnut oil
2 hot green chillis, deseeded
  and thinly sliced
25 g/1 oz roughly
  chopped coriander
2 tbsp freshly chopped mint

125 g/4 oz cucumber,
  finely chopped
40 g/1½ oz beansprouts
40 g/1½ oz roasted peanuts,
  roughly chopped

Put the noodles into a large bowl. Bring the stock to the boil and immediately pour over the noodles. Leave to soak for 4 minutes, or according to the packet directions. Drain well, discarding the stock or saving it for another use. Mix together the sesame oil and soy sauce and pour over the hot noodles. Toss well to coat and leave until cold.

Trim and thinly slice four of the spring onions. Heat the wok over a low heat and then add the oil. Add the spring onions and, as soon as they sizzle, remove from the heat and leave to cool. When cold, toss with the noodles.

On a chopping board, cut the remaining spring onions lengthways four to six times, then leave in a bowl of cold water until tassels form. Serve the noodles in individual bowls, each dressed with a little chilli, coriander, mint, cucumber, beansprouts and peanuts. Garnish with the spring onion tassels and serve.

Try This: FOR AN ALTERNATIVE: 178 FOR THE BARBECUE GRILL: 60

Crispy Noodle Salad

SERVES 4

2 tbsp sunflower seeds
2 tbsp pumpkin seeds
50 g/2 oz rice vermicelli
   or stir-fry noodles
175 g/6 oz unsalted butter
2 tbsp sesame seeds,
   lightly toasted

125 g/4 oz red cabbage,
   trimmed and shredded
1 orange pepper, deseeded
   and finely chopped
125 g/4 oz button
   mushrooms, wiped
   and quartered

2 spring onions, trimmed
   and finely chopped
salt and freshly ground
   black pepper
shredded pickled sushi
   ginger, to garnish

Preheat the oven to 200°C/400°F/Gas Mark 6, then sprinkle the sunflower and pumpkin seeds on a baking sheet. Toast in the oven, stirring occasionally, for 10–15 minutes or until lightly toasted. Remove from the oven and leave to cool.

Crush the rice vermicelli into small pieces (this is easiest in a plastic bag or while the noodles are still in the packet), and reserve. Melt the butter in a small saucepan and leave to cool for a few minutes. Pour the clear yellow liquid carefully into a bowl, leaving behind the white milky solids. Discard the milky solids.

Heat the yellow, clarified butter in a wok and fry the crushed noodles in batches until browned, stirring constantly and gently. Remove the fried noodles as they cook, using a slotted spoon, and drain on absorbent kitchen paper. Transfer the noodles to a bowl and add the toasted seeds.

Mix together the red cabbage, orange pepper, button mushrooms and spring onions in a large bowl and season to taste with salt and pepper. Just before serving, add the noodles and seeds to the salad and mix gently. Garnish with a little sushi ginger and serve.

Try This: FOR AN ALTERNATIVE: 216   FOR THE BARBECUE GRILL: 56

Cooked Vegetable Salad with Satay Sauce

SERVES 4

125 ml/4 fl oz groundnut oil
225 g/8 oz unsalted peanuts
1 onion, peeled and
    finely chopped
1 garlic clove, peeled
    and crushed
½ tsp chilli powder
1 tsp ground coriander
½ tsp ground cumin
½ tsp sugar

1 tbsp dark soy sauce
2 tbsp fresh lemon juice
2 tbsp light olive oil
salt and freshly ground
    black pepper
125 g/4 oz French
    green beans, trimmed
    and halved
125 g/4 oz carrots
125 g/4 oz cauliflower florets

125 g/4 oz broccoli florets
125 g/4 oz Chinese leaves or
    pak choi, trimmed and
    shredded
125 g/4 oz beansprouts
1 tbsp sesame oil

To garnish:
sprigs of fresh watercress
cucumber, cut into slivers

Heat a wok, add the oil, and when hot, add the peanuts and stir-fry for 3–4 minutes. Drain on absorbent kitchen paper and leave to cool. Blend in a food processor to a fine powder.

Place the onion and garlic, with the spices, sugar, soy sauce, lemon juice and olive oil in a food processor. Season to taste with salt and pepper, then process into a paste. Transfer to a wok and stir-fry for 3–4 minutes.

Stir 600 ml/1 pint hot water into the paste and bring to the boil. Add the ground peanuts and simmer gently for 5–6 minutes or until the mixture thickens. Reserve the satay sauce.

Cook the vegetables in batches in lightly salted boiling water. Cook the French beans, carrots, cauliflower and broccoli for 3–4 minutes, and the Chinese leaves or pak choi and beansprouts for 2 minutes. Drain each batch, drizzle over the sesame oil and arrange on a large warmed serving dish. Garnish with watercress sprigs and cucumber. Serve with the satay sauce.

 Try This: FOR AN ALTERNATIVE: 214 FOR THE BARBECUE GRILL: 104

Summer Desserts

Fruit Salad

SERVES 4

125 g/4 oz caster sugar
3 oranges
700 g/1½ lb lychees,
    peeled and stoned
1 small mango
1 small pineapple
1 papaya

4 pieces stem ginger
    in syrup
4 tbsp stem ginger syrup
125 g/4 oz Cape
    gooseberries or physallis
125 g/4 oz strawberries,
    hulled

½ tsp almond essence

To decorate:
lime zest
mint leaves

Place the sugar and 300 ml/½ pint of water in a small pan and heat, gently stirring until the sugar has dissolved. Bring to the boil and simmer for 2 minutes. Once a syrup has formed, remove from the heat and allow to cool.

Using a sharp knife, cut away the skin from the oranges, then slice thickly. Cut each slice in half and place in a serving dish with the syrup and lychees.

Peel the mango, then cut into thick slices around each side of the stone. Discard the stone and cut the slices into bite-sized pieces and add to the syrup.

Using a sharp knife again, carefully cut away the skin from the pineapple. Remove the central core using the knife or an apple corer, then cut the pineapple into segments and add to the syrup.

Peel the papaya, then cut in half and remove the seeds. Cut the flesh into chunks, slice the ginger into matchsticks and add with the ginger syrup to the fruit in the syrup.

Prepare the Cape gooseberries, by removing the thin, papery skins and rinsing lightly. Halve the strawberries, add to the fruit with the almond essence and chill for 30 minutes. Scatter with mint leaves and lime zest to decorate and serve.

Try This: FOR AN ALTERNATIVE: 228 FOR THE BARBECUE GRILL: 38

Orange Freeze

SERVES 4

4 large oranges
about 300 ml/½ pint low-fat
    vanilla ice cream
225 g/8 oz raspberries

75 g/3 oz icing sugar, sifted
redcurrant sprigs,
    to decorate

Set the freezer to rapid freeze. Using a sharp knife carefully cut the lid off each orange. Scoop out the flesh from the orange, discarding any pips and thick pith. Place the shells and lids in the freezer and chop any remaining orange flesh.

Whisk together the orange juice, orange flesh and vanilla ice cream, until well blended. Cover and freeze, for about 2 hours, occasionally breaking up the ice crystals with a fork or a whisk. Stir the mixture from around the edge of the container into the centre, then level and return to the freezer. Do this 2–3 times then leave until almost frozen solid.

Place a large scoop of the ice cream mixture into the frozen shells. Add another scoop on top, so that there is plenty outside of the orange shell and return to the freezer for 1 hour.

Arrange the lids on top and freeze for a further 2 hours, until the filled orange shell is completely frozen solid.

Meanwhile, using a nylon sieve press the raspberries into a bowl using the back of a wooden spoon and mix together with the icing sugar. Spoon the raspberry coulis on to four serving plates and place an orange at the centre of each. Dust with icing sugar and serve decorated with the redcurrants. Remember to return the freezer to its normal setting.

Try This: FOR AN ALTERNATIVE: 234   FOR THE BARBECUE GRILL: 50

Tipsy Tropical Fruit

SERVES 4

225 g/8 oz can pineapple
  chunks in natural juice
2 fairly ripe guavas
1 ripe papaya
2 ripe passion fruit
25 g/1 oz unsalted butter

1 tbsp orange juice
50 g/2 oz creamed coconut,
  chopped
50 g/2 oz soft light brown
  sugar
2 tbsp malibu liqueur or

white rum
sprigs of fresh mint, to
  decorate
vanilla ice-cream, to serve

Drain the pineapple chunks, reserving the juice. Pat the pineapple dry on absorbent kitchen paper. Peel the guavas and cut into wedges. Halve the papaya and scoop out the black seeds. Peel and cut into 2.5 cm/1 inch chunks. Halve the passion fruit and scoop out the seeds into a small bowl.

Heat the butter in a wok, add the pineapple and stir-fry over a high heat for 30 seconds. Turn down the heat and add the guavas and papaya. Drizzle over the orange juice and cook for 2 minutes, stirring occasionally, taking care not to break up the fruit.

Using a slotted spoon, remove the fruit from the wok, leaving any juices behind and transfer to a warmed serving dish. Add the creamed coconut to the wok with the sugar and pineapple juice. Simmer for 2–3 minutes, stirring until the coconut has melted.

Add the malibu or white rum to the wok and heat through, then pour over the fruit. Spoon the passion fruit pulp on top and serve hot with spoonfuls of ice-cream decorated with a sprig of mint.

Try This: FOR AN ALTERNATIVE: 224   FOR THE BARBECUE GRILL: 80

Summer Pavlova

SERVES 6–8

4 medium egg whites
225 g/8 oz caster sugar
1 tsp vanilla essence
2 tsp white wine vinegar
1½ tsp cornflour

300 ml/½ pint half-fat
    Greek-set yogurt
2 tbsp honey
225 g/8 oz strawberries,
    hulled

125 g/4 oz raspberries
125 g/4 oz blueberries
4 kiwis, peeled and sliced
icing sugar, to decorate

Preheat the oven to 150°C/300°F/Gas Mark 2. Line a baking sheet with a sheet of greaseproof or baking parchment paper.

Place the egg whites in a clean grease-free bowl and whisk until very stiff. Whisk in half the sugar, vanilla essence, vinegar and cornflour, continue whisking until stiff. Gradually, whisk in the remaining sugar, a teaspoonful at a time until very stiff and glossy.

Using a large spoon, arrange spoonfuls of the meringue in a circle on the greaseproof paper or baking parchment paper.

Bake in the preheated oven for 1 hour until crisp and dry. Turn the oven off and leave the meringue in the oven to cool completely.

Remove the meringue from the baking sheet and peel away the parchment paper. Mix together the yogurt and honey. Place the pavlova on a serving plate and spoon the yogurt into the centre.

Scatter over the strawberries, raspberries, blueberries and kiwis. Dust with the icing sugar and serve.

Try This: FOR AN ALTERNATIVE: 232   FOR THE BARBECUE GRILL: 72

Summer Pudding

SERVES 4

450 g/1 lb redcurrants
125 g/4 oz caster sugar
350 g/12 oz strawberries,
    hulled and halved
125 g/4 oz raspberries

2 tbsp Grand Marnier
    or Cointreau
8–10 medium slices white
    bread, crusts removed
mint sprigs, to decorate

low-fat Greek-set yogurt or
    low-fat fromage frais,
    to serve

Place the redcurrants, sugar and 1 tablespoon of water in a large saucepan. Heat gently until the sugar has just dissolved and the juices have just begun to run.

Remove the saucepan from the heat and stir in the strawberries, raspberries and the Grand Marnier or Cointreau.

Line the base and sides of a 1.1 litre/2 pint pudding basin with two thirds of the bread, making sure that the slices overlap each other slightly.

Spoon the fruit with their juices into the bread-lined pudding basin, then top with the remaining bread slices.

Place a small plate on top of the pudding inside the pudding basin. Ensure the plate fits tightly, then weigh down with a clean can or some weights and chill in the refrigerator overnight.

When ready to serve, remove the weights and plate. Carefully loosen round the sides of the basin with a round-bladed knife. Invert the pudding on to a serving plate, decorate with the mint sprigs and serve with the yogurt or fromage frais.

Try This: FOR AN ALTERNATIVE: 230   FOR THE BARBECUE GRILL: 88

Caramelised Oranges in an Iced Bowl

SERVES 4

For the iced bowl:
about 36 ice cubes
fresh flowers and fruits

8 medium-sized oranges
225 g/8 oz caster sugar
4 tbsp Grand Marnier
   or Cointreau

Set freezer to rapid freeze. Place a few ice cubes in the base of a 1.7 litre/3 pint freezable glass bowl. Place a 900 ml/1½ pint glass bowl on top of the ice cubes. Arrange the flower heads and fruits in between the two bowls, wedging in position with the ice cubes. Weigh down the smaller bowl with some heavy weights, then carefully pour cold water between the two bowls making sure that the flowers and the fruit are covered. Freeze for at least 6 hours or until the ice is frozen solid.

When ready to use, remove the weights and using a hot damp cloth rub the inside of the smaller bowl with the cloth until it loosens sufficiently for you to remove the bowl. Place the larger bowl in the sink or washing-up bowl, half filled with very hot water. Leave for about 30 seconds or until the ice loosens. Take care not to leave the bowl in the water for too long otherwise the ice will melt. Remove the bowl and leave in the refrigerator. Return the freezer to its normal setting.

Thinly pare the rind from two oranges and then cut into julienne strips. Using a sharp knife cut away the rind and pith from all the oranges, holding over a bowl to catch the juices. Slice the oranges, discarding any pips and reform each orange back to its original shape. Secure with cocktail sticks, then place in a bowl.

Heat 300 ml/½ pint water, orange rind and sugar together in a pan. Stir the sugar until dissolved. Bring to the boil. Boil for 15 minutes, until it is a caramel colour. Remove pan from heat. Stir in the liqueur, pour over the oranges. Allow to cool. Chill for 3 hours, turning the oranges occasionally. Spoon into the ice bowl and serve.

Try This: FOR AN ALTERNATIVE: 226   FOR THE BARBECUE GRILL: 86

Raspberry Sorbet Crush

SERVES 4

225 g/8 oz raspberries,
 thawed if frozen
grated rind and juice
 of 1 lime

300 ml/½ pint orange juice
225 g/8 oz caster sugar
2 medium egg whites

Set the freezer to rapid freeze. If using fresh raspberries pick over and lightly rinse.
Place the raspberries in a dish and, using a masher, mash to a chunky purée.

Place the lime rind and juice, orange juice and half the caster sugar in a large
heavy-based saucepan. Heat gently, stirring frequently, until the sugar is dissolved.
Bring to the boil and boil rapidly for about 5 minutes.

Remove the pan from the heat and pour carefully into a freezable container. Leave to
cool, then place in the freezer and freeze for 2 hours, stirring occasionally to break up
the ice crystals.

Fold the ice mixture into the raspberry purée with a metal spoon and freeze for a further
2 hours, stirring occasionally.

Whisk the egg whites until stiff. Then gradually whisk in the remaining caster sugar
a tablespoon at a time until the egg white mixture is stiff and glossy.

Fold into the raspberry sorbet with a metal spoon and freeze for 1 hour. Spoon into tall
glasses and serve immediately. Remember to return the freezer to its normal setting.

Try This: FOR AN ALTERNATIVE: 238   FOR THE BARBECUE GRILL: 70

Coconut Sorbet
with Mango Sauce

SERVES 4

2 sheets gelatine
250 g/9 oz caster sugar
600 ml/1 pint coconut milk

2 ripe mangos, peeled,
   pitted and sliced
2 tbsp icing sugar

zest and juice of 1 lime

Set the freezer to rapid freeze, 2 hours before freezing the sorbet. Place the sheets of gelatine in a shallow dish, pour over cold water to cover and leave for 15 minutes. Squeeze out excess moisture before use.

Meanwhile, place the caster sugar and 300 ml/½ pint of the coconut milk in a heavy-based saucepan and heat gently, stirring occasionally, until the sugar has dissolved. Remove from the heat.

Add the soaked gelatine to the saucepan and stir gently until dissolved. Stir in the remaining coconut milk. Leave until cold.

Pour the gelatine and coconut mixture into a freezable container and place in the freezer. Leave for at least 1 hour, or until the mixture has started to form ice crystals. Remove and beat with a spoon, then return to the freezer and continue to freeze until the mixture is frozen, beating at least twice more during this time.

Meanwhile, make the sauce. Place the sliced mango, icing sugar and the lime zest and juice in a food processor and blend until smooth. Spoon into a small jug.

Leave the sorbet to soften in the refrigerator for at least 30 minutes before serving. Serve scoops of sorbet on individual plates with a little of the mango sauce poured over. Remember to turn the freezer to normal setting.

Try This: FOR AN ALTERNATIVE: 236   FOR THE BARBECUE GRILL: 98

Stir–fried Bananas & Peaches
with Rum Butterscotch Sauce

SERVES 4

2 medium-firm bananas
1 tbsp caster sugar
2 tsp lime juice
4 firm, ripe peaches
 or nectarines

1 tbsp sunflower oil

**For the rum
 butterscotch sauce:**
50 g/2 oz unsalted butter

50 g/2 oz soft light
 brown sugar
125 g/4 oz demerara sugar
300 ml/½ pint double cream
2 tbsp dark rum

Peel the bananas and cut into 2.5 cm/1 inch diagonal slices. Place in a bowl and sprinkle with the caster sugar and lime juice and stir until lightly coated. Reserve.

Place the peaches or nectarines in a large bowl and pour over boiling water to cover. Leave for 30 seconds, then plunge them into cold water and peel off their skins. Cut each one into 8 thick slices, discarding the stone.

Heat a wok, add the oil and swirl it round the wok to coat the sides. Add the fruit and cook for 3–4 minutes, shaking the wok and gently turning the fruit until lightly browned. Spoon the fruit into a warmed serving bowl and clean the wok with absorbent kitchen paper.

Add the butter and sugars to the wok and stir continuously over a very low heat until the sugar has dissolved. Remove from the heat and leave to cool for 2–3 minutes.

Stir the cream and rum into the sugar syrup and return to the heat. Bring to the boil and simmer for 2 minutes, stirring continuously until smooth. Leave for 2–3 minutes to cool slightly, then serve warm with the stir-fried peaches and bananas.

 Try This: FOR AN ALTERNATIVE: 242   FOR THE BARBECUE GRILL: 104

Stuffed Amaretti Peaches

SERVES 4

4 ripe peaches
grated zest and juice
 of 1 lemon
75 g/3 oz Amaretti biscuits
50 g/2 oz chopped blanched

almonds, toasted
50 g/2 oz pine nuts, toasted
40 g/1½ oz light
 muscovado sugar
50 g/2 oz butter

1 medium egg yolk
2 tsp clear honey
crème fraîche or Greek
 yogurt, to serve

Prepare the barbecue (covered if available), or preheat the oven to 180°C/350°F/Gas Mark 4. Halve the peaches and remove the stones. Take a very thin slice from the bottom of each peach half so that it will sit flat. Dip the peach halves in lemon juice and arrange on 4 squares of kitchen foil big enough to fold into parcels round each peach, or in a baking tray (to be used in the barbecue or oven).

Crush the Amaretti biscuits lightly and put into a large bowl. Add the almonds, pine nuts, sugar, lemon zest and butter. Work with the fingertips until the mixture resembles coarse breadcrumbs. Add the egg yolk and mix well until the mixture is just binding.

Divide the Amaretti and nut mixture between the peach halves, pressing down lightly. Fold up the foil, if using, and cook on the barbecue, or in the covered barbecue or preheated oven for 15 minutes, or until the peaches are tender and the filling is golden. Remove from the barbecue or oven and drizzle with the honey.

Place two peach halves on each serving plate and spoon over a little crème fraîche or Greek yogurt, then serve.

Try This: FOR AN ALTERNATIVE: 240   FOR THE BARBECUE GRILL: 74

Caramelised Chocolate Tartlets

SERVES 6

350 g/12 oz ready-made shortcrust pastry, thawed if frozen
150 ml/¼ pint coconut milk
40 g/1½ oz demerara sugar
50 g/2 oz plain dark chocolate, melted
1 medium egg, beaten
few drops vanilla essence
1 small mango, peeled, stoned and sliced
1 small papaya, peeled, deseeded and chopped
1 star fruit, sliced
1 kiwi, peeled and sliced, or use fruits of your choice

Preheat the oven to 200˚C/400˚F/Gas Mark 6, 15 minutes before baking. Lightly oil six individual tartlet tins. Roll out the ready-made pastry on a lightly floured surface and use to line the oiled tins. Prick the bases and sides with a fork and line with non-stick baking parchment and baking beans. Bake blind for 10 minutes in the preheated oven, then remove from the oven and discard the baking beans and the baking parchment.

Reduce the oven temperature to 180˚C/350˚F/Gas Mark 4. Heat the coconut milk and 15 g/½ oz of the sugar in a heavy-based saucepan, stirring constantly until the sugar has dissolved. Remove the saucepan from the heat and leave to cool.

Stir the melted chocolate, the beaten egg and the vanilla essence into the cooled coconut milk. Stir until well mixed, then strain into the cooked pastry cases. Place on a baking sheet and bake in the oven for 25 minutes or until set. Remove and leave to cool, then chill in the refrigerator.

Preheat the grill, then arrange the fruits in a decorative pattern on the top of each tartlet. Sprinkle with the remaining demerara sugar and place the tartlets in the grill pan. Grill for 2 minutes or until the sugar bubbles and browns. Turn the tartlets, if necessary and take care not to burn the sugar. Remove from the grill and leave to cool before serving.

Try This: FOR AN ALTERNATIVE: 234 FOR THE BARBECUE GRILL: 54

Summer Drinks

Summer Special Soda

Non-Alcoholic

SERVES 2

85 ml/3 fl oz orange juice
½ small, ripe gallia melon
175 g/6 oz fresh raspberries
1 tsp finely grated
   orange rind
2 scoops good quality
   vanilla ice cream,
   to serve
soda water, to serve
orange zest, to decorate

Summer is a time full of lush fruits and vegetables, bursting with sun, vitamins and flavour. Make sure that the fruits you use are perfectly ripe for maximum taste and flavour.

Place the orange juice in a smoothie machine or blender.

Peel the melon, discard the seeds and cut the flesh into chunks.
Add to the smoothie machine or blender with the raspberries and orange rind.

If using a smoothie machine, blend on mix for 15 seconds and then on smooth for 45 seconds. In a blender, blend for 1–2 minutes or until smooth.

Pour into glasses and place a scoop of ice cream in each glass.

Top up with soda water and serve immediately, sprinkled with a little orange zest.

Alternative Try using raspberry ripple or chocolate ice cream in place of the vanilla, or a combination of both.

Try This: FOR AN ALTERNATIVE: 250   FOR AN ALCOHOLIC DRINK: 236

Tangy Summer Sensation

 Non-Alcoholic

SERVES 2

½ cantaloupe melon
1 ripe papaya
175 g/6 oz carrots
4 tbsp orange juice
4 ice cubes
2 mint sprigs, to decorate

Bursting with colour and full of tangy flavours, this smoothie
is bound to be a big hit at any time of the year.

Peel the melon and papaya, discard the seeds, and cut into chunks.
Reserve two pieces of papaya for decoration.

Cut the carrots into chunks.

Place all the ingredients in a smoothie machine or blender with the ice cubes.

If using a smoothie machine, blend on mix for 15 seconds and then on smooth
for 45 seconds. In a blender, blend for 1–2 minutes or until smooth.

Pour into glasses, decorate and serve.

Alternative Add four fresh, ripe, stoned apricots if available in place of the papaya.

Try This: FOR AN ALTERNATIVE: 248   FOR AN ALCOHOLIC DRINK: 308

Banana & Raspberry Smoothie

SERVES 2-3

2 ripe bananas
225 g/8 oz fresh raspberries
75 g/3 oz tofu, drained
150 ml/¼ pint orange juice
4 ice cubes

This nourishing smoothie will help sustain you throughout the day. Not only is it full of energy-rich fruits, it also contains tofu which will keep you feeling energized.

Peel the bananas and cut into chunks. Place the bananas in a smoothie machine or blender.

Reserve two raspberries for decoration then place all the remaining ingredients into the smoothie machine or blender.

If using a smoothie machine, blend on mix for 15 seconds and then on smooth for 45 seconds. In a blender, blend for 1–2 minutes or until smooth.

Pour into glasses, decorate and serve.

Alternative Other fruits can be used in place of the raspberries – try blueberries, tayberries or loganberries.

Try This: FOR AN ALTERNATIVE: 254   FOR AN ALCOHOLIC DRINK: 346

Peanut Butter Bliss

Non-Alcoholic

SERVES 2

4 tbsp orange juice
3 tbsp crunchy or smooth
   peanut butter
1 ripe banana, chopped
2 tbsp lemon juice
2 scoops chocolate ice cream
2 scoops vanilla ice cream,
   to serve
fan wafer biscuits, to serve

It is your choice whether you use crunchy peanut butter or smooth in this recipe. Although relatively high in calories, an occasional treat is a good idea as it helps to lift the spirits and give a general feeling of well-being. Nuts also contain important nutrients.

Place the orange juice, peanut butter, banana, lemon juice and chocolate ice cream in a smoothie machine or blender.

If using a smoothie machine, blend on mix for 15 seconds and then on smooth for 45 seconds. In a blender, blend for 1–2 minutes or until smooth.

Pour into glasses and add a scoop of vanilla ice cream to each glass and put a wafer biscuit in each scoop. Serve immediately.

Alternative Replace the ice cream with scoops of frozen strawberry yogurt or raspberry sorbet.
and add a few fresh strawberries or raspberries to the machine prior to blending.

Try This: FOR AN ALTERNATIVE: 288 FOR AN ALCOHOLIC DRINK: 300

Frosty Fruit Smoothie

Non-Alcoholic

SERVES 2

175 g/6 oz chilled,
   seedless green grapes
2 ripe passion fruits
½ small ogen or
   cantaloupe melon,
   chilled
150 ml/¼ pint chilled
   apple juice
4 ice cubes

During the summer months when a cold frosty smoothie is called for, it is a good idea to keep a variety of fruits in the refrigerator, so that a refreshing drink can be whizzed up in seconds.

Rinse the grapes and discard any stalks. Reserve a few for decoration and place the remainder in a smoothie machine or blender.

Scoop the flesh and seeds from the passion fruits, sieve if a smooth texture is preferred, and add to the machine.

Discard the skin and seeds from the melon and cut into chunks.

Place all the remaining ingredients in the machine. If using a smoothie machine, blend on mix for 15 seconds and then on smooth for 45 seconds. In a blender, blend for 1–2 minutes or until smooth.

Pour into cold glasses, decorate and serve.

Alternative Other chilled juices can be used in place of the apple juice. Apple and cranberry or apple and mango juice work particularly well.

Try This: FOR AN ALTERNATIVE: 268 FOR AN ALCOHOLIC DRINK: 342

Tropical Fruit Smoothie

Non-Alcoholic

SERVES 2-3

1 large, ripe avocado
2 tbsp lime juice
1 medium, ripe pineapple
1 tsp clear honey
150 ml/¼ pint chilled
   coconut milk
4 ice cubes
2–3 scoops chocolate ice
   cream, to serve

Pineapple contains bromelain which helps to balance the acidity and alkalinity levels in the digestive system. Although coconut milk contains saturated fat, research indicates that it is not nearly as harmful as fat from animal and dairy products.

Peel the avocado, discard the stone, cut the flesh into chunks and sprinkle with the lime juice.

Cut the plume and skin off the pineapple and discard. Cut into quarters and discard the hard central core. Cut the flesh into chunks.

Place all the ingredients except the ice cream in a smoothie machine or blender. If using a smoothie machine, blend on mix for 15 seconds and then on smooth for 45 seconds. In a blender, blend for 1–2 minutes or until smooth.

Pour into glasses, top with the ice cream and serve immediately.

Alternative Omit the pineapple and use any other tropical fruits instead. Papayas, passion fruits or mangos would all work well in this recipe.

Try This: FOR AN ALTERNATIVE: 266   FOR AN ALCOHOLIC DRINK: 344

Chilly Cherry

Non-Alcoholic

SERVES 4

500 g pack frozen mixed
  fruits containing cherries,
  blackberries, raspberries
  and strawberries,
  beginning to thaw
300 ml/½ pint apple and
  cranberry juice
2 spoonfuls frozen raspberry
  or lemon sorbet
4 mint sprigs, to decorate
8 thawed or fresh cherries,
  to decorate

Growing cherries can be very labour intensive, which is most probably why they are one of the most expensive fruits available. They are seldom seen frozen, normally only found in packs of mixed frozen fruits – don't be put off using these packs. They provide all the nutrients you would get from ripe fruits and are a great standby for long, hot summer days.

Place all the ingredients in a smoothie machine or blender.

If using a smoothie machine, blend on mix for 15 seconds and then on smooth for 45 seconds. In a blender, blend for 1–2 minutes or until smooth and 'slushy'.

Pour into glasses and serve immediately, topped with mint sprigs and some fresh or thawed cherries.

Alternative Use packs of single fruits, such as raspberries or even cranberries. Cranberries may need a little clear honey to sweeten, as they are very tart when ripe.

Try This: FOR AN ALTERNATIVE: 262 FOR AN ALCOHOLIC DRINK: 312

Strawberry Slush

 Non-Alcoholic

SERVES 4

450 g/1 lb fresh
   strawberries, hulled
1 tbsp balsamic vinegar
3 tbsp orange juice
4 ice cubes
4 mint sprigs, to decorate

Strawberries are now readily available all year round, coming from many countries worldwide. When locally grown strawberries are available, use these however, as the flavour will be far superior to those that have been picked slightly under-ripe. Locally grown berries are allowed to ripen on the plant, thus enjoying more of the sun, and have much more flavour.

Lightly rinse the strawberries and reserve 4 for decoration. Leave the remaining strawberries to drain. Place on a tray and sprinkle with the balsamic vinegar and leave for at least 5 minutes.

Place the strawberries and any juice together with the orange juice and ice cubes in a smoothie machine or blender.

If using a smoothie machine, blend on mix for 15 seconds and then on smooth for 45 seconds. In a blender, blend for 1–2 minutes or until smooth and a 'slush' is formed.

Pour into glasses, decorate and serve immediately.

Alternative Look for white balsamic vinegar in place on the traditional balsamic vinegar. Or use a few twists of freshly ground black pepper instead.

Try This: FOR AN ALTERNATIVE: 270 FOR AN ALCOHOLIC DRINK: 342

Summer Cooler

Non-Alcoholic

SERVES 4

1 large wedge of watermelon
100 g/4 oz ripe strawberries
1 ripe banana
3 tbsp elderflower cordial
few sprigs fresh coriander
4 ice cubes

When it is hot and sunny, there are times when all you want is a long, cool drink to help you unwind and relax. Try this – guaranteed to cool you down in seconds.

Discard the skin and seeds from the watermelon and cut into chunks.

Lightly rinse the strawberries and peel the banana, cutting it into large chunks.

Place the fruits and elderflower cordial with the ice cubes in a smoothie machine or blender.

If using a smoothie machine, blend on mix for 15 seconds and then on smooth for 45 seconds. In a blender, blend for 1–2 minutes or until smooth and a 'slush' is formed.

Pour into glasses and serve immediately. If liked, add a few extra ice cubes to each glass

Alternative In place of the ice cubes, add two large scoops of strawberry ice cream before blending.

Try This: FOR AN ALTERNATIVE: 274 FOR AN ALCOHOLIC DRINK: 320

Eastern Delight

SERVES 2

300 ml/½ pint coconut milk
400 g can lychees, drained
2 cardamom pods
1 lemon grass stalk
1 small piece star anise
2 scoops vanilla ice cream,
   to serve
2 lemon slices, to decorate

Canned lychees are blended with Eastern spices in this recipe
to make an aromatic smoothie with a hint of the Orient.

Place the coconut milk with the drained fruits in a smoothie machine or blender.

Place the cardamom pods in a pestle and pound with a mortar to remove the seeds.
Place the seeds in the machine.

Remove the outer leaves from the lemon grass, chop, then pound with the star
anise until as fine as possible. Add to the machine.

If using a smoothie machine, blend on mix for 15 seconds and then on smooth
for 45 seconds. In a blender, blend for 1–2 minutes or until smooth.

Pour into glasses, top with the ice cream,
decorate and serve immediately.

Alternative You will find that the small pieces of spice will sink to the bottom of the drink, but you can sieve the liquid if wanted.
Use live natural yogurt in place of the coconut milk if preferred.

Try This: FOR AN ALTERNATIVE: 258   FOR AN ALCOHOLIC DRINK: 346

Fragrant Peach Smoothie

SERVES 2

2 ripe peaches
2 ripe passion fruits
300 ml/½ pint peach and
    passion fruit yogurt
few drops vanilla extract
2 scoops raspberry or
    strawberry ice cream,
    to serve

Both peaches and nectarines are available as white and yellow fleshed varieties, the yellow varieties being the most common. Whichever you use, do ensure that the fruit is at it best – ripe and juicy.

Cut the peaches in half, discard the stones and place in a smoothie machine or blender.

Reserve half a passion fruit. Scoop out the flesh and seeds from the remaining passion fruits and sieve if a smoother texture is preferred.

Add the scooped passion fruit to the machine with the yogurt and vanilla extract.

If using a smoothie machine, blend on mix for 15 seconds and then on smooth for 45 seconds. In a blender, blend for 1–2 minutes or until smooth.

Pour into glasses and top with the ice cream. Spoon a little of the reserved passion fruit flesh and seeds on top and serve.

Alternative Nectarines, apricots and plums can be used here in place of the peaches. Do ensure that the fruits are ripe but not bruised.

Try This: FOR AN ALTERNATIVE: 272   FOR AN ALCOHOLIC DRINK: 332

Almond, Plum and Strawberry Smoothie

 Non-Alcoholic

SERVES 2

225 g/8 oz ripe plums
300 ml/½ pint bio
　strawberry yogurt
few drops almond essence
2–3 tsp clear honey,
　or to taste
2 scoops strawberry or
　vanilla ice cream, to serve
2 strawberry slices,
　to decorate
1 tbsp toasted flaked
　almonds, to decorate

Plums offer a good source of fibre. Red plums also contain beta carotene – the pigment found in foods such as carrots, oranges and dark green vegetables – and an important antioxidant nutrient.

Rinse the plums, cut in half, discard the stones and place in a smoothie machine or blender.

Spoon the yogurt into the machine and add the almond essence and honey to taste.

If using a smoothie machine, blend on mix for 15 seconds and then on smooth for 45 seconds. In a blender, blend for 1–2 minutes or until smooth.

Pour into glasses, add a scoop of ice cream to each, top with a strawberry slice, sprinkle with the toasted flaked almonds and serve.

Alternative If fresh plums are not available, use a 400 g can of preserved plums. Drain well and then proceed as above.

Try This: FOR AN ALTERNATIVE: 252　FOR AN ALCOHOLIC DRINK: 342

Passionate Peach Melba Smoothie

Non-Alcoholic

SERVES 2

1 ripe passion fruit
3 tbsp mango or orange juice
3–4 ripe peaches, stoned
175 g/6 oz fresh or thawed
　frozen raspberries
4 scoops vanilla ice cream
4 peach wedges, to decorate
fan wafer biscuits, to serve

Like the dessert of the same name, this smoothie is quick and easy to make and tastes even better than it looks. As with all smoothies, it is important to ensure that the fruit you use is in peak condition.

Reserve 4 raspberries for decoration. Cut the passion fruit in half and scoop out the flesh and seeds. Sieve the flesh if a smoother texture is preferred.

Place the passion fruit in a smoothie machine or blender and add the mango or orange juice, peaches, remaining raspberries and two scoops of ice cream.

If using a smoothie machine, blend on mix for 15 seconds and then on smooth for 45 seconds. In a blender, blend for 1–2 minutes or until smooth.

Pour into glasses and add a scoop of ice cream to each, with a couple of raspberries and wedge of peach. Top with a wafer and serve.

Alternative Make the smoothie as above, omitting the raspberries but adding more peaches and a little more ice cream. Top with the ice cream, drizzle with raspberry coulis and serve immediately.

 Try This: FOR AN ALTERNATIVE: 268   FOR AN ALCOHOLIC DRINK: 332

Real Strawberry Milkshake

 Non-Alcoholic

SERVES 2

225 g/8 oz ripe strawberries
300 ml/½ pint chilled
semi-skimmed milk
4 ice cubes
2 scoops strawberry
flavoured ice cream,
to serve
1 tbsp lightly whipped
whipping or double
cream, to serve
2 extra ripe strawberries,
to decorate
mint sprigs, to decorate

Whether or not this transports you back to childhood,
once tasted this fabulous shake will have you hooked.

Hull the strawberries and rinse lightly. Place in a smoothie machine or blender and
add the milk and ice cubes.

If using a smoothie machine, blend on mix for 15 seconds and then on smooth for
45 seconds. In a blender, blend for 1–2 minutes or until smooth.

Pour into tall glasses and add a scoop of ice cream to each, top with a little
whipped cream and decorate with the extra strawberry and mint sprig.

Alternative Other fruits can be used in the same way. Try bananas, raspberries, apricots or pineapple, varying the flavour of
ice cream accordingly. Or make a chocolate milkshake by omitting all the fruits and using 2–3 tbsp of melted chocolate.

Try This: FOR AN ALTERNATIVE: 270 FOR AN ALCOHOLIC DRINK: 346

Kiwi, Cucumber & Orange

Non-Alcoholic

SERVES 2

2 ripe kiwi fruits
4 tbsp apple juice
1 hothouse cucumber
2 blood oranges
4 ice cubes
a handful of raspberries
6 tbsp crème fraîche
2 fruit kebabs using gold
   kiwi and blueberries,
   to decorate

It really does not matter whether you use green or gold kiwi fruits in this recipe – both will work very well. If you can find blood oranges use these, as they will give a distinctive flavour to this smoothie.

Peel the kiwi fruits and cut into chunks, then place in a smoothie machine or blender, together with the apple juice.

Peel the cucumber, discarding the seeds, chop and add to the machine.

Peel the oranges, discarding the bitter white pith and any pips. Add to the machine together with the ice cubes and raspberries.

If using a smoothie machine, blend on mix for 15 seconds and then on smooth for 45 seconds. In a blender, blend for 1–2 minutes or until smooth.

Add the crème fraîche and whizz for a further 20 seconds.
Pour into glasses and serve decorated with the fruit kebabs.

Alternative If blood oranges are unavailable, look for a fruit juice made from blood oranges or use traditional-style oranges.

Try This: FOR AN ALTERNATIVE: 250   FOR AN ALCOHOLIC DRINK: 344

Greek Delight

Non-Alcoholic

SERVES 2

4 ripe figs
2–3 tsp clear honey,
   or to taste
2 large oranges
150 ml/¼ pint Greek yogurt
150 ml/¼ pint
   semi-skimmed milk
2 scoops vanilla ice cream,
   to serve
2 mint sprigs, to decorate

Enjoy a taste of the Mediterranean sun with Greek yogurt and plump, lush purple or green figs. There is no need to skin these, but do use ripe fruits and if necessary allow to ripen for a couple of days in a warm room.

Lightly rinse the figs and cut in half, then place in a smoothie machine or blender with honey to taste.

Peel the oranges, discarding the bitter white pith, and divide into segments. Add to the machine.

Add the yogurt and milk.

If using a smoothie machine, blend on mix for 15 seconds and then on smooth for 45 seconds. In a blender, blend for 1–2 minutes or until smooth.

Pour into glasses, add a scoop of ice cream to each and decorate with a sprig of mint. Serve immediately.

Alternative Use 150 ml/¼ pint freshly squeezed orange juice in place of the whole oranges.

Try This: FOR AN ALTERNATIVE: 288   FOR AN ALCOHOLIC DRINK: 330

Blueberry Cooler

SERVES 2

150 g/5 oz fresh blueberries
1–2 tsp caster sugar
150 ml/¼ pint clear
    apple juice
300 ml/½ pint live
    natural yogurt
4 ice cubes
2 scoops raspberry ripple ice
    cream, to serve
2 mint sprigs, to decorate

Blueberries are grown on small, low lying bushes in hot climates such as Umbria and parts of the United States. Recent research has shown that they have strong antioxidant properties, even more so with dried blueberries.

Rinse the blueberries and reserve a few for decoration. Place the rest in a smoothie machine or blender with the sugar, apple juice, yogurt and ice cubes.

If using a smoothie machine, blend on mix for 15 seconds and then on smooth for 45 seconds. In a blender, blend for 1–2 minutes or until a 'slush' is formed.

Pour into glasses and add the ice cream. Decorate with the reserved blueberries and the mint sprigs and serve.

Alternative Pour the prepared Blueberry Cooler into a freezeable container and freeze on rapid freeze for 30 minutes or until semi-frozen. Spoon into tall glasses and serve with a long spoon.

Try This: FOR AN ALTERNATIVE: 260   FOR AN ALCOHOLIC DRINK: 318

Summer Sizzler

SERVES 2

1 medium, ripe pineapple
3 tbsp pineapple juice
1 ripe passion fruit
100 g/4 oz fresh strawberries
2–3 tsp clear honey
150 ml/¼ pint bio
    strawberry yogurt
4 ice cubes
mint sprigs to decorate

When using yogurt in a smoothie take care not to over-blend, as the yogurt can lose its consistency and become quite thin. Therefore when using yogurt with fruits that take a little more effort to blend, add the yogurt towards the end.

Discard the plume, skin and central core from the pineapple and cut into chunks. Place in a smoothie machine or blender with the pineapple juice.

Scoop the flesh and seeds from the passion fruit. Add to the machine.

Lightly rinse the strawberries and cut any large strawberries in half. Add to the machine with the honey, yogurt and ice cubes.

If using a smoothie machine, blend on mix for 15 seconds and then on smooth for 45 seconds. In a blender, blend for 1–2 minutes or until smooth.

Pour into glasses. Decorate the glasses with the reserved strawberries and mint sprigs then serve immediately.

Alternative Other fruits and flavoured yogurts can be used in place of the strawberries. Try raspberries, blackberries, mango, guava or blueberries.

Try This: FOR AN ALTERNATIVE: 264   FOR AN ALCOHOLIC DRINK: 348

Caribbean Slush

SERVES 2

2 ripe papayas
1 ripe mango
300 ml/½ pint chilled
    pineapple juice
small piece root ginger
4 ice cubes
2 pineapple wedges,
    to decorate

Enjoy this cooling drink when the heat is up and you are relaxing round a pool, in the garden or just need a cool down.

Peel the papaya, discard the seeds and cut the flesh into chunks.

Peel the mango and cut the flesh away from the stone, chop the flesh and place in a smoothie machine or blender with the papaya flesh and pineapple juice.

Peel the ginger, grate and add to the machine with the ice cubes.

If using a smoothie machine, blend on mix for 15 seconds and then on smooth for 45 seconds. In a blender, blend for 1–2 minutes or until a 'slush' is formed.

Pour into chilled glasses, decorate with the pineapple wedges and serve immediately.

Alternative Replace the root ginger with a little finely grated lime rind and two tablespoons of lime juice.

Try This: FOR AN ALTERNATIVE: 250 FOR AN ALCOHOLIC DRINK: 332

Orange & Chocolate Smoothie

Non-Alcoholic

SERVES 2

1 large orange
300 ml/½ pint chilled
    semi-skimmed milk
50 g/2 oz good quality plain
    or milk chocolate, grated
4 scoops chocolate ice cream

If you are a real chocoholic, you will love this smoothie. Do use the best chocolate and ice cream that you can find and don't worry about the calories – you need a treat every now and again.

Grate 1–2 teaspoons of orange rind from the orange and reserve. Using a zester remove a few strands of orange zest for decoration and reserve.

Peel the orange, discarding the bitter white pith, and divide into segments. Place the orange rind and segments in a smoothie machine or blender with the milk and grated chocolate and two scoops of ice cream.

If using a smoothie machine, blend on mix for 15 seconds and then on smooth for 45 seconds. In a blender, blend for 1–2 minutes or until smooth.

Pour into glasses and add a scoop of ice cream to each, decorate with the orange zest and serve.

Alternative Use vanilla ice cream in place of the chocolate ice cream and sprinkle with a little grated chocolate before serving.

Try This FOR AN ALTERNATIVE: 288   FOR AN ALCOHOLIC DRINK: 294

Toffee & Chocolate Smoothie

Non-Alcoholic

SERVES 2

300 ml/½ pint toffee
   flavoured yogurt
150 ml/¼ pint chilled
   semi-skimmed milk
4 scoops vanilla ice cream
2 rolled wafer biscuits,
   to serve
1 tsp crumbled chocolate
   flake, to decorate
2 fan wafer biscuits,
   to serve

This is definitely an indulgent smoothie – so have it in the summer when you can go for a walk to work off the excess calories.

Place the yogurt, milk and two scoops of the ice cream in a smoothie machine or blender.

If using a smoothie machine, blend on mix for 15 seconds and then on smooth for 45 seconds. In a blender, blend for 1–2 minutes or until smooth.

Pour into chilled glasses and add the remaining scoop of ice cream to each along with a wafer biscuit. Sprinkle with the chocolate flake and serve.

Alternative Use a different flavoured yogurt in place of the toffee: try raspberry, cherry or peach and passion fruit.

Try This: FOR AN ALTERNATIVE: 286   FOR AN ALCOHOLIC DRINK: 302

Virgin Mary

Non-Alcoholic

SERVES 1

4 ice cubes
5 measures tomato juice
½–1 tsp Tabasco
1–2 dashes Worcestershire
    sauce
1 tsp freshly squeezed
    lemon juice
celery stick and lemon twist,
    to garnish

As the name suggests this is the alcohol free version of a 'Bloody Mary'.
When poured into the glass, garnished with the celery stick and with the
dash or two of Worcestershire sauce, it looks as good as any cocktail.

Place the ice cubes into a short tumbler and pour over the tomato juice.

Add the Tabasco to taste together with the Worcestershire sauce and lemon juice.

Stir well until mixed then serve garnished with the celery stick and lemon twist.

Alternative If liked make this a tall drink. Half fill a tall glass with crushed ice and pour in the tomato juice. Add the Tabasco and
Worcestershire sauces to taste together with the lemon juice and top up with soda water. Use the celery stick as the stirrer.

Try This: FOR AN ALTERNATIVE: 260 FOR AN ALCOHOLIC DRINK: 292

Bloody Mary

Alcoholic

SERVES 1

1 measure vodka
3 measures tomato juice
½ tsp lemon juice
2 dashes Worcestershire
   sauce
3–4 dashes Tabasco
pinch each of salt and freshly
   ground black pepper
celery stick as a stirrer
lemon slice to garnish

Reputed to have been devised in Harry's Bar, New York, in 1921 it became
all the rage in 1931 once prohibition had ended.

Place all the ingredients except the celery and garnish into a cocktail shaker and
shake for 1 minute.

Strain into an old-fashioned glass and add the celery stick to use as a stirrer
and garnish with a lemon slice.

Alternative Place some ice cubes if liked in the glass before pouring the cocktail over. Replace the vodka with gin
– this is known as Red Snapper.

Try This: FOR AN ALTERNATIVE: 294 FOR A NON-ALCOHOLIC DRINK: 290

Screwdriver

Alcoholic

SERVES 1

4 ice cubes, crushed
2 measures vodka
4 measures freshly
    squeezed orange juice
1 small slice of orange
    and 1 maraschino cherry
    to garnish

There are a few theories as to the origins of the name of this famous cocktail. One is that a US oilman stationed in Iran was seen stirring his drink with his screwdriver, hence the name.

Place all the ingredients except the garnish into a chilled cocktail glass and stir with a bar spoon.

Garnish with the orange slice and cherry then serve.

Alternatives The vodka can be replaced with either rum or gin and become a Screwdriver Rum or Screwdriver Gin.

Try This: FOR AN ALTERNATIVE: 304   FOR A NON-ALCOHOLIC DRINK: 248

Frozen Daiquiri

Alcoholic

SERVES 1

225 g/8 oz white granulated sugar
150 ml/¼ pt water
4 ice cubes, crushed
freshly squeezed juice from 2 ripe limes
2 measures white rum
lime wedge to garnish

Developed in Cuba around 1896 this very popular classic cocktail can be found on most bar menus. Try some of the other delicious variations that can be found.

To make sugar syrup: place the sugar and water in a heavy-based saucepan and place over a gentle heat; heat gently, stirring occasionally until the sugar has completely dissolved; bring to the boil and boil steadily (to a temperature of 105˚C/221˚F) until a light syrup is formed; remove from the heat. Leave to cool, then pour into a screw-top sterilized bottle. When cold, screw down the lid. Use as required. It is best to make the syrup in small amounts and use it freshly made, as it can start to crystallize after a while.

Place the crushed ice into a cocktail shaker and pour in the lime juice, sugar syrup and white rum.

Shake for 1 minute or until the shaker feels very cold. Strain into the chilled glass and serve garnished with the lime wedge.

Alternative Try a Melon Daiquiri by adding 2 measures of Midori (Melon Liqueur) and only use 1 measure of freshly squeezed lime juice.

Try This: FOR AN ALTERNATIVE: 324   FOR A NON-ALCOHOLIC DRINK: 256

Salty Dog

Alcoholic

SERVES 1

2 measures gin
4 measures grapefruit juice
4–5 ice cubes, broken
1 lime slice to garnish

Give this cocktail a touch of sparkle by adding a Margarita twist to the drink and frost the edge of the glass with grapefruit juice and salt. Allow it to dry before using.

Frost the glass with table salt: place a small amount of salt in a saucer as wide as the glass; dip the rim of the glass in water or egg white, shake off the excess and place it in the salt; press down until well coated, and allow to dry before using.

Pour the gin and grapefruit juice into a cocktail shaker and shake for 30 seconds.

Place the broken ice into a tumbler and strain in the gin and grapefruit.

Garnish and serve immediately.

Alternative To make a Greyhound serve in a plain glass. Replace the gin with vodka.

Try This: FOR AN ALTERNATIVE: 300   FOR A NON-ALCOHOLIC DRINK: 250

Between the Sheets

Alcoholic

SERVES 1

4 ice cubes, crushed
1½ measures brandy
1 measure white rum
½ measure Cointreau
1 tsp freshly squeezed
   lemon juice
1 tsp sugar syrup
   (*see* page 296)
lemon butterfly twist
   to garnish

Often a cocktail is served chilled but without the ice being present in the serving glass. This is achieved by placing the ingredients and crushed ice into a cocktail shaker and then shaking until a frost forms on the outside. The cocktail is then strained into the glass.

Place the crushed ice with the brandy, white rum, Cointreau, lemon juice and sugar syrup in a cocktail shaker.

Shake for 1 minute or until thoroughly chilled and a frost appears on the outside of the shaker.

Strain into a cocktail glass, garnish and serve.

Alternative Leave out the sugar syrup for a cocktail with more bite.

Try This: FOR AN ALTERNATIVE: 306   FOR A NON-ALCOHOLIC DRINK: 248

Sea Breeze

 Alcoholic

SERVES 1

1 measure vodka
2–3 measures (or to taste)
cranberry juice
1–2 measures (or to taste)
grapefruit juice
4 ice cubes
orange slice and fresh
  cranberries if available,
  to garnish

Back in the 1930s this cocktail was made with gin, grenadine and lemon juice. However, over the years it has developed into this very popular, and has to be said, delicious cocktail.

Place the vodka in a cocktail shaker and add the cranberry and grapefruit juice to taste.

Shake until blended.

Place the ice into a tumbler, pour the cocktail over and serve garnished with an orange slice and a stirrer.

Alternative Replace the grapefruit juice with pineapple juice to make a Bay Breeze.

Try This: FOR AN ALTERNATIVE: 298   FOR A NON-ALCOHOLIC DRINK: 260

Harvey Wallbanger

Alcoholic

SERVES 1

6–8 ice cubes
½ measure Galliano
1½ measures vodka
5 measures freshly
   squeezed orange juice
2 small orange wedges
   to garnish

There are a few stories regarding the naming of this famous drink. One of them relates to Harvey, a Californian surfer who added Galliano to a Screwdriver – he loved it so much he ordered quite a few. On trying to leave he bounced and bumped his way out from one wall to the next until he found the door – hence the Harvey Wallbanger was born.

Place some ice cubes into a collins glass (a tall clear tumbler that holds about 28 cl/10 fl oz) and pour over the Galliano.

Place the vodka, orange juice and remaining ice into a cocktail shaker and shake until frosty.

Strain then pour over the Galliano, garnish and serve with a stirrer.

Alternative If liked pour the chilled vodka and orange over crushed ice then carefully pour the Galliano on top so it floats on the surface.

Try This: FOR AN ALTERNATIVE: 294   FOR A NON-ALCOHOLIC DRINK: 250

Rum Planter Cocktail

Alcoholic

SERVES 1

4 ice cubes, crushed
1 measure dark rum
1 tsp freshly squeezed
    orange juice
1 tsp freshly squeezed
    lemon juice
2 dashes Angostura Bitters
1 tsp caster sugar
tropical fruits to garnish,
    such as pineapple,
    mango and banana

When a recipe calls for a little freshly squeezed citrus fruit, simply cut a small or medium sized wedge of fruit and place in a hand-held squeezer or simply just squeeze using your fingers.

Place the crushed ice into a cocktail shaker and add the rum with the orange and lemon juice, together with the Angostura Bitters and sugar.

Shake for 1 minute or until a frost is formed on the outside of the shaker.

Pour into a tumbler and garnish with small pieces of pineapple, mango and banana.

Alternative Vary the fruits used for garnish. For a special occasion make a stunning garnish by threading small pieces of mango, kiwi, pineapple and papaya on to a short kebab stick and balance across the glass.

Try This: FOR AN ALTERNATIVE: 310   FOR A NON-ALCOHOLIC DRINK: 248

Tequila Sunrise

Alcoholic

SERVES 1

4 ice cubes
½ measure grenadine
2 measures tequila
120 ml/4 fl oz freshly
    squeezed orange juice
orange slice and maraschino
    cherry to garnish

As the name suggests, this cocktail originated in Mexico around 1930.
It was called Tequila Sunrise most probably due to the colours that are caught
in the glass, which are similar to the beautiful sunrises found in Mexico.

Place the crushed ice into a tall tumbler, then slowly pour the grenadine over the ice allowing
it to sink to the bottom of the glass.

Place the tequila and orange juice into a cocktail shaker and blend for 30 seconds.

Strain into the glass and serve garnished with an orange slice,
maraschino cherry and a straw.

Alternative Try a Florida Sunrise, simply replace the orange juice with pineapple juice and garnish with a small wedge of pineapple.

Try This: FOR AN ALTERNATIVE: 342 FOR A NON-ALCOHOLIC DRINK: 272

Zombie

Alcoholic

SERVES 1

3 ice cubes
1 measure dark rum
1 measure white rum
½ measure apricot brandy
2 measures pineapple juice
2 measures freshly
squeezed orange juice
1 measure lime juice
wedge of pineapple,
maraschino cherry and
mint sprig to garnish

Created in 1933 in America's very first South Sea Island restaurant in order to complement the exotic food that was to be served there. It quickly became a great hit and other similar beach restaurants quickly sprang up.

Place the ice into a cocktail shaker then pour in the other ingredients.

Shake for 30 seconds then pour into a tall glass and garnish with a pineapple wedge, cherry and mint sprig.

Serve immediately and add a straw to the glass.

Alternative If liked frost the rim of the glass with lime juice and salt (*see page 298*).

Try This: FOR AN ALTERNATIVE: 306   FOR A NON-ALCOHOLIC DRINK: 284

Bacardi Classic

SERVES 1

1½–2 measures Bacardi rum
1 measure lemon juice
1 tsp grenadine
1 tsp, or to taste, sugar syrup
 (*see* page 296)
2 ice cubes, crushed
1 maraschino cherry

It was in 1936 that a New York hotel bar and restaurant started serving this cocktail and without using Bacardi rum. After a visit by the makers of Bacardi rum, to the courts a temporary injunction was raised and later that year became permanent at the Supreme Court which stated that ONLY Bacardi rum should be used for this cocktail.

Place all the ingredients into a cocktail shaker and shake for 30 seconds.

Pour into a cocktail glass and serve garnished with the cherry on a cocktail stick.

Alternative Use the two measures of Bacardi rum if a stronger drink is preferred and replace the lemon juice with lime juice.

Try This: FOR AN ALTERNATIVE: 310 FOR A NON-ALCOHOLIC DRINK: 276

Brandy Classic

Alcoholic

SERVES 1

1 measure brandy
1 measure blue curaçao
1 tbsp freshly squeezed
lemon juice
1 tbsp syrup from a jar of
maraschino cherries
3 ice cubes, crushed
lemon rind spiral and
maraschino cherry
to garnish

This cocktail gets its colour by the addition of blue curaçao. This attractive liqueur comes from the dried peel of the green orange that is grown in the Caribbean island of the same name.

Place the ingredients into a cocktail shaker and shake for 30 seconds.

Pour into a cocktail glass and serve garnished with the lemon rind spiral and a maraschino cherry.

Alternatives Try replacing the brandy with either gin or vodka or even white rum.

Try This: FOR AN ALTERNATIVE: 300   FOR A NON-ALCOHOLIC DRINK: 268

French Leave

SERVES 1

2 ice cubes, crushed
2 measures vodka
1 measure Pernod
1 measure freshly
   squeezed orange juice
maraschino cherry,
   mint sprig and peach
   slice to garnish

Pernod is made from the spice star anise that can be found in North Vietnam and Southern China. It is an aromatic spice used extensively in these areas to flavour many traditional dishes as well as drinks.

Place the ingredients into a cocktail shaker and blend for 30 seconds or until a frost forms on the outside of the shaker.

Strain into a cocktail glass and serve, garnish with a maraschino cherry, mint sprig and peach slice.

Alternative Replace the vodka with either brandy or gin.

Try This: FOR AN ALTERNATIVE: 304   FOR A NON-ALCOHOLIC DRINK: 264

Black Widow

Alcoholic

SERVES 1

3 ice cubes
2 measures dark rum
1–1½ measures
   Southern Comfort
freshly squeezed lime juice
1 tsp sugar syrup
   (*see* page 296)
lime slice

This cocktail has a definite kick to it and is not for the faint-hearted, combining the fruity flavours of peach and orange with a distinct hint of herbs and a good splash of Southern Comfort. Guaranteed to get any party going.

Place the ice cubes into a cocktail shaker with all the other ingredients.

Shake for 30 seconds then strain into a cocktail glass and serve garnished with the lime slice.

Alternative Try a slice of lemon, rather than lime, as garnish.

Try This: FOR AN ALTERNATIVE: 326   FOR A NON-ALCOHOLIC DRINK: 280

Skipper

SERVES 1

3 ice cubes
½ measure grenadine
1 measure dry vermouth
3–4 measures Scotch whisky
freshly squeezed juice
    from ½ orange,
    preferably organic
orange twist to garnish

There are many brands of Scotch whisky blends to choose from, so when using whisky for cocktails use whichever you prefer, but I would advise drinking the malts without accompaniment.

Place the ice cubes into a cocktail shaker and add the grenadine, dry vermouth, whisky and orange juice.

Shake for about 30 seconds then pour into a short tumbler and serve garnished with the orange twist.

Alternative Look out for Skipper's Ripper – a rather different drink containing cola, granadine, rum and Southern Comfort.

Try This: FOR AN ALTERNATIVE: 312   FOR A NON-ALCOHOLIC DRINK: 274

Caipirinha

SERVES 1

1 lime
1½–2 tsp caster sugar
4 ice cubes, broken
2 measures cachaça

Caipirinha is the national cocktail of Brazil and is normally made with the country's favourite brandy, cachaça, which is made from sugar cane. The name means 'peasant's drink'. It is made directly in the glass, never in a cocktail shaker.

Cut the lime into small wedges and place with the sugar into an old-fashioned glass (a stubby glass with a thick base, cut glass or clear, that holds about 23 cl/8fl oz).

Using a spoon crush the lime wedges and sugar together until the juice flows out of the lime.

Add sufficient broken ice to fill the glass then top up with the cachaça and serve.

Alternative Many varieties of this cocktail are served the length and breadth of Brazil. These are often served with a variety of fruits in place of the lime. Try passion fruits, kiwi, pineapple, summer berries or grapes. Sometimes soy or dairy milk is added giving a creamy cocktail. Another alternative can be made by using vodka.

Try This: FOR AN ALTERNATIVE: 324   FOR A NON-ALCOHOLIC DRINK: 276

Mojito

Alcoholic

SERVES 1

4 ice cubes, crushed
2–3 mint sprigs
2 measures white rum
3 tbsp freshly squeezed
    lime juice
2 tsp (or to taste)
    demerara sugar
soda water
fresh mint sprig to garnish

One of the most popular summer cocktails around today. This Cuban drink has become the 'wow' both in London and New York regardless of the weather. There are many variations and part of the fun is experimenting with the ingredients to discover which ones best suit your taste buds.

Place half the crushed ice into a glass and add the mint sprigs. Carefully crush the mint on the ice.

Pour the rum, lime juice, sugar and remaining ice into a cocktail shaker and shake until a frost forms on the outside.

Pour the shaker's contents into the glass, top up with soda water, garnish with a fresh mint sprig and serve with a stirrer.

Alternative Try using other flavoured rums such as dark rum or even fruit-flavoured rums, such as mango flavoured.

 Try This: FOR AN ALTERNATIVE: 322 FOR A NON-ALCOHOLIC DRINK: 266

Mint Julep

Alcoholic

SERVES 1

4 ice cubes, crushed
4 fresh mint sprigs
1 measure sugar syrup
   (*see* page 296)
3 measures bourbon
2–3 fresh mint sprigs
   to garnish

The word 'julep' is thought to have come from an ancient Arabic word meaning 'rose water'. It was not until the eighteenth century that the first mention of julep occurred in the United States and it quickly caught on, so that by the nineteenth century it had been thoroughly Americanized.

Place the mint sprigs into a tumbler and add the sugar syrup. With the back of a bar spoon gently crush the mint and sugar syrup to extract the mint flavour. Remove the crushed sprigs.

Slowly stir in the bourbon then add the crushed ice.

Place the fresh mint with the stalks down and the leaves facing upwards into the glass. Serve with a straw.

Alternative Some Mint Juleps are served without crushing the mint and sugar syrup together. Simply fill a tumbler with crushed ice and pour over the sugar syrup then slowly stir in the bourbon. Add the mint sprigs and serve.

 Try This: FOR AN ALTERNATIVE: 328   FOR A NON-ALCOHOLIC DRINK: 256

Jungle Juice

SERVES 1

4 ice cubes, crushed
2 whole ice cubes
1 measure Pisang Ambon
½ measure brandy
1 measure gin
4 measures freshly
   squeezed orange juice
2 tsp freshly squeezed
   lemon juice
3 mint sprigs

Pisang Ambon is a very sweet, bright green liqueur from Indonesia and is made from herbs and green bananas. It works well when blended with orange juice or orange flavoured liqueur such as Cointreau.

Place all the ingredients into a cocktail shaker except for the crushed ice.

Shake for 1 minute or until a frost forms on the outside of the cocktail shaker.

Strain into a tumbler then add the ice cubes, the mint sprigs with the leaves pointing up, and serve.

Alternative Add 1 measure of Cointreau to the above cocktail and top the glass up with soda water.

  Try This: FOR AN ALTERNATIVE: 326   FOR A NON-ALCOHOLIC DRINK: 258

Classic
Champagne Cocktail

Alcoholic

SERVES 1

2 dashes Angostura Bitters
1 sugar cube
3 measures chilled freshly
    opened champagne
½ measure cognac
orange twist to garnish

The origin of this cocktail remains a mystery but is thought to have been created around 1850 in the American South. In 1888 a cocktail competition was organized by a US journalist and the winner was a John Doherty who produced this recipe, which he claimed came from a Southern US State.

Place the sugar cube into a champagne flute and shake the Angostura Bitters bottle over the sugar cube.

Pour in the champagne and cognac and stir lightly.

Garnish with an orange twist and serve immediately.

Alternative If liked add a squeeze of lemon or orange before adding the champagne and cognac. Use the same fruit that has been squeezed into the cocktail as a garnish.

Try This: FOR AN ALTERNATIVE: 332   FOR A NON-ALCOHOLIC DRINK: 274

Bellini

Alcoholic

SERVES 1

2 measures vodka
½ measure peach schnapps
1 tsp peach juice
chilled freshly opened
  champagne to top up
peach slice to garnish

When making a champagne cocktail it is important that the champagne has been chilled and opened just before drinking for maximum pleasure. When storing champagne it is best to store the bottle horizontally so as the wine is kept in contact with the cork – this prevents the cork from drying out.

Pour the vodka, peach schnapps and peach juice into a cocktail shaker and shake for 20 seconds.

Pour into a chilled champagne flute then top up with the chilled champagne.

Serve immediately, garnished with the peach slice.

Alternative Use puréed peach instead of schnapps and peach juice, for a slightly thicker, less alcoholic drink.

Try This: FOR AN ALTERNATIVE: 330   FOR A NON-ALCOHOLIC DRINK: 268

John Collins

 Alcoholic

SERVES 1

4 ice cubes, crushed
2 measures bourbon
1 measure freshly
   squeezed lemon juice
½ measure sugar syrup
   (*see* page 296)
chilled soda water to top up
lemon slice to garnish

A Collins is an ideal drink for the hot weather. Normally it is not shaken but made and served in a tall glass with a spirit such as bourbon, plus lemon or lime juice, sugar syrup (*see* page 296) and topped up with soda water.

Place the ice cubes in a chilled tall glass such as a highball glass (a tall tumbler, normally clear, that holds 28 cl/10 fl oz).

Pour over the bourbon, the lemon juice and sugar syrup.

Stir with a swizzle stick then top up with soda water, garnish with a lemon slice and serve.

Alternative   There are many variations to a John Collins. Try a Rum Collins by replacing the bourbon with rum – or a Mint Collins – here replace the bourbon with vodka and add a measure of crème de menthe.

Try This: FOR AN ALTERNATIVE: 318   FOR A NON-ALCOHOLIC DRINK: 290

Singapore Sling

Alcoholic

SERVES 1

3 ice cubes, crushed
1 measure gin
1 measure cherry brandy
½ measure Benedictine
½ measure freshly
   squeezed lime juice
4 measures freshly
   squeezed orange juice
soda water to top up
small wedge pineapple and
   a fresh cherry, to garnish

There are two ways of making a Sling: either make the cocktail then pour into an ice-filled glass or all the ingredients can be shaken together in a cocktail shaker, except for the soda water then strained into a glass.

Pour the gin, cherry brandy and Benedictine into a cocktail shaker.

Strain in the lime and orange juice and shake for 30 seconds or until blended.

Place the ice cubes into a collins glass (*see* page 304) and pour over the cocktail.

Top up with soda water, add a swizzle stick and garnish with the pineapple wedge and cherry.

Alternative A Raffles Singapore Sling is not topped up with soda water and is a short drink unlike the Singapore Sling.

Try This: FOR AN ALTERNATIVE: 320   FOR A NON-ALCOHOLIC DRINK: 270

Vodka Twist Fizz

Alcoholic

SERVES 1

2 ice cubes
2 tbsp freshly squeezed
  lime juice
½ tsp sugar syrup
  (*see* page 296)
1 medium egg white,
preferably organic
3 dashes Pernod
3 measures vodka
ginger ale to top up
lime slice to garnish

A Fizz is similar to a Collins but is always shaken before the fizz is added. It normally does not contain very much ice so as not to inhibit the fizz of the drink. Normally served in the morning or at midday with a swizzle stick and a straw.

Place the ice cubes into a cocktail shaker and strain in the lemon juice.

Add the sugar syrup with the egg white, Pernod and vodka.

Shake for 45 seconds or until well blended and a frost starts to form on the outside of the shaker.

Pour into a chilled highball glass (*see* page 334) half-filled with ice and top up with ginger ale.

Garnish with the lime slice and add a straw and a swizzle stick.

Alternative If liked replace the Pernod and ginger ale with grenadine and soda water and add the freshly squeezed juice from 1 small orange.

Try This: FOR AN ALTERNATIVE: 348   FOR A NON-ALCOHOLIC DRINK: 250

Margarita

SERVES 1

1 measure freshly
   squeezed lemon juice
1 tbsp salt
2 measures tequila
1½ measures triple sec
½ measure blue curaçao
½ measure freshly
   squeezed lemon juice

The story is that the Margarita was created in the late 1940s for the well-known actress, Marjorie King, as she was allergic to all spirits except for tequila. There are many variations on the classic recipe, all of which are delicious.

Frost the glass with salt (*see* page 298) and allow to dry.

Place the tequila in a cocktail shaker with the triple sec, blue curaçao and ½ measure of lemon juice.

Shake for 30 seconds until blended, pour into the frosted glass and serve.

Alternative Replace the blue curaçao and the triple sec with 1 measure of green curaçao or Galliano. To make a Frozen Margarita fill a glass with crushed ice and pour over the shaken cocktail.

Frozen Fruit Margarita

Alcoholic

SERVES 1

1 measure freshly
squeezed lemon juice
1 tbsp caster sugar
1½ measures tequila
1 measure strawberry
liqueur
½ measure triple sec
3 ice cubes, crushed
1 fresh strawberry fan

These are really simple to make and provide a delicious fruity drink, absolutely perfect for relaxing and having fun. Try experimenting with your favourite fruits and mixer liqueurs.

Frost the glass with salt (*see* page 298) and allow it to dry.

Place the tequila with the remaining lemon juice, strawberry liqueur and triple sec and add the crushed ice.

Shake for 30 seconds or until blended then pour into the glass and serve garnished with the strawberry fan.

Alternative Use Midori, Cointreau or Grand Marnier in place of the strawberry liqueur and garnish with the appropriate fruit.

Try This: FOR AN ALTERNATIVE: 340   FOR A NON-ALCOHOLIC DRINK: 262

Caribbean Sunset

Alcoholic

SERVES 1

3 ice cubes
1 measure crème de banane
½ measure blue curaçao
½ measure freshly squeezed
   lemon juice
½ measure mango juice
2 tbsp whipped cream
1 tsp grenadine
slice of star fruit and a
   small wedge of mango
   to garnish

This cocktail is so named as the colours reflect not only the glorious sunsets in the Caribbean, but the flavour and aromas from the Islands.

Place a couple of the ice cubes into a cocktail shaker and the remaining ice into a short glass.

Pour the crème de banane into the cocktail shaker together with the blue curaçao, the lemon and mango juice and half the whipped cream.

Shake for 30 seconds or until blended.

Pour over the ice cubes in the glass and add the grenadine allowing it to slowly sink.

Top with the remaining cream, garnish and serve.

Alternative Try adding ½ measure of gin for more bite.

Try This: FOR AN ALTERNATIVE: 348   FOR A NON-ALCOHOLIC DRINK: 284

Pina Colada

Alcoholic

SERVES 1

4 ice cubes, crushed
1 measure white rum
2 measures coconut cream
2 measures pineapple juice
pineapple wedge and
      maraschino cherry
      to garnish

This exotic cocktail originates in Puerto Rico and the name means 'strained pineapple juice'. You can use the pineapple juice from a can of pineapple or use fresh pineapple juice that will include the fruit fibres unless it is strained after blending in a liquidizer. Do make sure that the pineapple used is fresh and perfectly ripe. When served the whole drink should be milky white with no hint of separation.

Place the crushed ice into a cocktail shaker and pour in the white rum, coconut cream and pineapple juice.

Shake for 20 seconds or until well blended.

Strain into a tall glass and garnish with the pineapple wedge and cherry, and serve with a straw.

Alternative Increase and decrease the amounts of rum and pineapple juice to taste.

Try This: FOR AN ALTERNATIVE: 344   FOR A NON-ALCOHOLIC DRINK: 288

Frozen Key Lime

Alcoholic

SERVES 1

3 ice cubes
1 measure white rum
½ measure dark rum
1½ measures freshly
squeezed lime juice
1–2 scoops good
quality vanilla
ice cream
soda water to top up
little grated chocolate
to garnish

This could almost be regarded as a cross between a dessert and a drink as it is based on the very popular pudding – Key Lime Pie. Beware, the dessert does not have a kick like this has. Enjoy.

Place the ice into a cocktail shaker and pour in the white and dark rum together with the lime juice.

Shake for 30 seconds or until blended then strain into a tall glass and top up with the soda water.

Float the ice cream on top and sprinkle with the grated chocolate.

Serve with a straw and spoon if liked.

Alternative Use a mixture of citrus fruit juices rather than the lime juice and garnish with a twist from each.

Try This: FOR AN ALTERNATIVE: 338   FOR A NON-ALCOHOLIC DRINK: 278

Index